Copyright © 2017 SuperSummary

All rights reserved. No part of this publication may be reproduced, transmitted, or distributed in any form, by electronic or mechanical means, including photocopying, scanning, recording, or file sharing, without prior permission in writing from the publisher, except as provided by United States of America copyright law.

The purpose of this study guide is to provide supplemental educational material. It is not intended as a substitute or replacement of THE SAMURAI'S GARDEN.

Published by SuperSummary, www.supersummary.com

ISBN – 9781097246069

For more information or to learn about our complete library of study guides, please visit http://www.supersummary.com

Please submit any comments, corrections, or questions to:
http://www.supersummary.com/support/

TABLE OF CONTENTS

PLOT OVERVIEW	3
CHAPTER SUMMARIES AND ANALYSES	4
Autumn: September 15, 1937-Autumn: September 29, 1937	4
Autumn: October 5, 1937-Autumn: October 29, 1937	11
Autumn: October 30, 1937-Autumn: November 30, 1937	16
Autumn: December 1, 1937-Winter: December 7, 1937	22
Winter: December 21, 1937-Winter: February 4, 1938	29
Winter: February 5, 1938- Winter: March 14, 1938	32
Spring: March 28, 1938-Spring: May 30, 1938	37
Summer: June 6, 1938-Summer: July 5, 1938	43
Summer: July 9, 1938-Summer: August 16, 1938	46
Summer: August 17, 1938-Autumn: September 23, 1938	48
Autumn: September 28, 1938-Autumn: October 19	52
Autumn: October 20, 1938-Autumn: October 26, 1938	55
Autumn: October 27, 1938-Autumn: October 29, 1938	58
CHARACTER ANALYSIS	62
Stephen Chan	
Matsu	
Sachi	
Kenzo	
Tomoko	
Fumiko	
Ba-Ba	
Mah-mee	
Pie	
Anne and Henry	
Ching	
King	
Keiko	
Hiro	
Michiko	
THEMES	68
SYMBOLS AND MOTIFS	72
IMPORTANT QUOTES	76
ESSAY TOPICS	85

PLOT OVERVIEW

The Samurai's Garden tells the story of Stephen Chan, a 20-year-old Chinese painter, writer, and student who, at the urging of his upper-middle-class parents, leaves school in Canton to spend a year recuperating from an undisclosed illness at his family's beach house in Tarumi, Japan. The narrative present of the novel is set during the first year of the Second Sino-Japanese War (1937-1945).

The novel is character-driven. Stephen's traditional Chinese mother lives at the family home in Hong Kong with Stephen's sister Pie, with whom he is close; his Westernized father stays mainly at an apartment in Japan, on business, and is having an affair. As the Japanese army sweeps through China, Stephen becomes close to Matsu, the "samurai" who has long been the caretaker of the beach house and its garden, and Matsu's longtime love Sachi, who suffers from leprosy and lives in the nearby leper colony of Yamaguchi. Sachi and Matsu live lives haunted by suicide: there is Sachi's attempted seppuku; Matsu's sister Tomoko's successful seppuku, many years ago; and Matsu and Sachi's childhood friend Kenzo's hanging in present day. Stephen falls for a beautiful Tarumi villager named Keiko, but their relationship is doomed by their respective nationalities and her overbearing father.

Through these and other relationships, Stephen learns a great deal about life and death, love and commitment, solitude and connection, and the nature of happiness. The novel is Stephen's story, but as his months in Tarumi unfold, the stories of those around him – especially the triangle of Matsu, Sachi, and Kenzo – emerge. Stephen learns a number of things about the relationships of those around him: that Sachi and Kenzo were once engaged, that Sachi contracted leprosy, that Kenzo abandoned her, that

Sachi tried to commit family-honor seppuku but could not, and that Matsu saved and cared for her, then fathered her stillborn child. As Stephen learns these things, his own story gains dimension, and his family drama is put into perspective. He returns to Hong Kong uncertain of both his future and China's future, whole in body and changed in spirit.

Narrative and form are provided by Stephen's journal, which he introduces in the first "chapter" (all chapters are journal entries). These entries recount Stephen's present, along with flashbacks provided by the stories other characters tell him, along with his own memories. Stephen's writing is simple yet descriptive, honest, and both a record and a source of his transformation.

This introspective novel's relatively spare plot in the present allows it to soar backward and imagine forward with ease. Stephen's days in Tarumi are mostly uncomplicated: he visits the village and its places of worship; swims at the beach; becomes familiar with Yamaguchi and its people; corresponds with his family; spends time with Matsu, Sachi, and Keiko; gains physical strength; and creates art. On this canvas of the everyday, author Gail Tsukiyama paints the colorful, poignant, and sometimes life-shattering stories of her major and minor characters.

CHAPTER SUMMARIES AND ANALYSES

Autumn: September 15, 1937-Autumn: September 29, 1937

Autumn: September 15, 1937 Summary

The novel opens during the first year of the Second Sino-Japanese War. Stephen Chan, a thin, wavy-haired 20-year-old Chinese student and oil painter, introduces his method of storytelling: a newly purchased book of Japanese parchment paper in which he will record his journey of recovery from an unknown illness. Stephen contracts this illness in the spring, while studying at Lingan University in Canton. After two weeks of argument, Stephen has convinced his stubborn, short, bespectacled and tightly-suited import-export businessman father, "Ba-Ba," to allow him to travel alone from the apartment his father keeps in Kobe, Japan to his grandfather's beach house in the village of Tarumi.

Stephen notes that his father, with homes in both China and Japan, "makes his life in both places and the way he bows low with eyes averted seems at times more Japanese than Chinese to me" (4). This sense of duality continues in the Western names Stephen's father has given to all of the children – Stephen; Penelope ("Pie," twelve years old); Anne (the elder sister); and Henry (the younger brother). Stephen's father is affectionate and overprotective; he sees Stephen's painting as a time-wasting hobby.

Before his trip to Tarumi, Stephen recounts the story of his illness so far.

When Stephen contracted his illness, he was sent away from university by his instructors. He traveled under the care of his friend King to his family's home in British-sovereign Hong Kong, where many Chinese were taking refuge in the streets from the Japanese invasion. There, through the hot summer, during which the Japanese captured Tientsin and surrounded Peking, Stephen's mother ("Mah-mee") and her servant Ching isolated and worried over him. He suffered coughs and fevers, which were first misdiagnosed by an English doctor as tuberculosis. Pie – round-eyed, pigtailed, intelligent, frail but feisty – was kept from entering his room; Anne and Henry return to school in Macao.

In August, as the Japanese invade Shanghai, where "a bloody standoff continues" (4), Stephen's father sends for him by letter, saying he will take him from Kobe to Tarumi, where the climate is drier. Ching, Stephen's mother's servant, travels with Stephen to Kobe, where she comments on the "Japanese devils" who have "driven our Chinese out of their homes" (5).

In Kobe, transportation and thus Ba-Ba's business have been interrupted by the war. Due to working long hours, Stephen's father is unable to take him to Tarumi as hoped. Instead, Michiyo, Stephen's father's servant, cares for him as one lonely week after another pass.

Having recounted the story of his illness so far, Stephen returns to his journey of recovery. Having convinced his father to allow him to go to Tarumi on his own, he packs light for the train and is on his way. His father asks if he has given Stephen enough money, warns him not to tire himself out with his painting, reminds him that he may contact him by phone at work, and pays a porter to look after him.

On the train ride to Tarumi, Stephen reflects on his recent solitude and the "fear and attraction of facing the unknown" (6). A little girl on the train reminds him of Pie, and he remembers her sneaking into his room in Hong Kong to whisper goodbye.

At the tiny village station in Tarumi, Stephen meets Matsu, a weathered, gray-haired man in his sixties who is the caretaker of his grandfather's beach house and lives there alone. Matsu's parents served Pao-Lin Chan, Stephen's grandfather, before Matsu did. Matsu has now served Chan for thirty years. Matsu is brusque, in sharp contrast to the women who've been fawning over Stephen. The two men walk briskly in the heat, over white sand and past the village, then past a number of bamboo-gated beach houses. They arrive at the house Stephen remembers from his childhood.

The traditional house and small grounds are lovely and harmonic, with a koi pond and bridge shaded by trees. At the door, the men follow the Japanese custom of replacing their shoes with slippers. Matsu runs an outdoor Japanese bath for Stephen, and Stephen washes before stepping into the steaming-hot cedar tub, which functions as a soothing transition: "when I sat perfectly still as Matsu advised, my body calmed. Matsu stood to the side and almost smiled as I leaned back, letting the hot water embrace me" (10-11).

Autumn: September 16, 1937 Summary

Stephen wakes in his room the next morning with his book across his chest, feeling healthier and hungry. He walks through the immaculate house, noting the traditional décor – *tatami* mats, *shoji* screens, *zabuton* cushions, and scroll paintings. One of the paintings, by his grandfather, is in a *tokonoma* (recessed alcove) in his room. It especially pleases him. He pauses in his grandfather's once-forbidden study, seeing his reflection in the lacquered desk.

After a simple breakfast and simpler conversation with Matsu (Stephen doesn't speak much Japanese), Stephen walks with his sketch pad down a sandy path to the wide beach. The other beach houses are empty in the off-season save for those inhabited by servants like Matsu. Stephen thinks of being alone: "I suppose I might get used to it, like an empty canvas you slowly begin to fill" (13).

Becoming hot after sketching the ocean and mountains, Stephen goes for a naked swim. The bracing cold and exercise give him energy and a sense of freedom. He floats, remembering his time in Hong Kong missing his friends while bedridden from illness. When he sees two girls on the beach, he wants to call out to them, glad to know other young people are in Tarumi. Remembering that he is naked, he lowers himself in the water until they are out of sight.

When Stephen returns to the house, Matsu is out. Stephen eats a lunch of udon and fish cake Matsu has left him and writes letters to his mother, Pie, and King. He does not know if his letter will reach King; the Japanese had not reached Canton when he heard from his friend last, but things may have changed. He recalls that King is one of the few of his friends who understands how important Stephen's painting is to him.

When Matsu returns with magazines and items to prepare for dinner, Stephen stands in the kitchen doorway and watches him. He notes how different this feels from his home in Hong Kong, where his Mah-mee doesn't enter the kitchen except to give instructions on what to serve at her mah-jongg games. As Matsu plucks a chicken, he asks

Stephen if he needs anything. Stephen inquires about young people staying in the area. Matsu says that the only young people left in this season live in the village.

Stephen asks Matsu if he gets lonely here and if he has friends with whom to pass the time. These are rather personal questions, but Stephen persists. Matsu tells Stephen that he gardens and reads magazines that his sister sends from Tokyo and that he has two sisters, one dead now. Stephen tells Matsu that he has two sisters and a brother, which Matsu, of course, already knows. Matsu clears his throat and turns away to continue cooking. Stephen remains: "Matsu didn't look up or say another word. Still, it was a start" (16).

Autumn: September 20, 1937 Summary

Stephen has been in Tarumi less than a week, but it feels longer to him. He gives up on a frustrating drawing session after a night of difficult sleep. He imagines that painting would be easier than drawing, but canvases his father promised to send from Kobe have not arrived, and his father will not be able to visit until the following week. There has been no word from his mother and Pie in Hong Kong.

Conversations with Matsu have become slightly more productive during the day, but Matsu spends most of his time at night in the kitchen or listening to classical music and news of the invasion on the radio. Stephen asks Matsu what he thinks about Japan's victories in China. Matsu responds, "Japan is like a young woman who thinks too much of herself. She's bound to get herself into trouble" (17).

Stephen swims every morning, hoping to see the girls from the beach again. So far, they have not appeared. He notices that, unlike himself, Matsu seems at peace in the quiet of the house.

Autumn: September 29, 1937 Summary

His loneliness continuing, Stephen resolves to become well through rest, exercise, and his art. As he returns from a morning swim, Matsu tells him that a package has arrived for him. Stephen discovers a parcel of canvases and a letter from his mother and Pie. He sits in the garden near the pond to read the letter.

Mah-mee inquires about his health, promises to visit, updates him on Anne and Henry in Macao, and speculates that the Japanese will not enter Hong Kong due to British sovereignty. As for Pie's portion of the letter, she is designing dresses like Shirley Temple's with her dressmaker, Anne has fainted and been resuscitated with brandy and smelling salts during a blackout, and Pie would like to faint in order to try some brandy. Stephen is at once comforted and troubled; he feels isolated from his family and the larger world.

Stephen closes his eyes to nap, then hears whispering voices outside the fence. He sees two shadows, then feels something brush against his head – a tossed shower of white petals. Hearing laughter, he darts to the gate and calls out to the two girls from the beach, who run away without looking back.

Autumn: September 15, 1937-Autumn: September 29, 1937 Analysis

The first five chapters of *The Samurai's Garden* establish Stephen's life before Tarumi, then his day-to-day life in Tarumi. We learn the basics of his family and school relationships and, through them, begin to understand Stephen's cultural, economic, and political contexts. His once-traditional country is westernizing: "my parents gave us all Christian names at birth, since my father believes it an asset in the business world to be addressed with ease by Westerners" (4). His family is privileged. His world is becoming polarized by war. Overarching all individual stories in the novel is this war, the Second Sino-Japanese, the largest Asian war of the 20th century. It began as a conflict between the Republic of China and the Empire of Japan and was ultimately resolved by the Japanese surrender to the Allies at the end of World War II. The Japanese army's encroachment on China is evident in Stephen's worries about, and delays in, communications with his family in Hong Kong and Kobe, in addition to his school friend King in Canton: "I had no idea if my letter would ever reach him there, with the Japanese swarming all over China" (14).

Isolation becomes apparent as a theme from the novel's outset. Stephen is isolated first by his illness, then by being a Chinese stranger in Tarumi: "For the past week, I've endured all the quiet and loneliness like a blanket covering me until I'm well again" (17). We learn that Matsu lives a fairly solitary life as well. As the servant and the son orbit each other, it seems their solitudes may begin to intersect, encouraging the hope of connection. The relationship between Stephen and Matsu, like those explored so far between Stephen and Ching and Stephen's family and Matsu's father, is predicated on service. This theme of service – its power dynamics and possibilities for transcendence – will entwine with the theme of isolation as Stephen's story continues.

The novel is highly visual, with detailed imagery revealing inner and outer worlds and supporting themes. A few motifs gain traction in the first five chapters. Food, like the udon and fish cake Matsu serves Stephen, is pleasant and grounding, a common language. Flowers, like the white petals tossed by the girls from the beach suggest grace in hard times. Stephen's journal and art are his sanctuaries, and his gifts during a period of global and personal change.

Weather and seasons establish themselves as symbolic in these chapters; changes in temperature, precipitation, and the local flora correspond directly with Stephen's inner journey. Autumn is cool and brings a sense of solitude to Tarumi with the exit of holiday travelers; the season is transitional, presaging the idea of death inherent in winter.

Autumn: October 5, 1937-Autumn: October 29, 1937

Autumn: October 5, 1937 Summary

Ba-Ba, Stephen's father, has arrived unexpectedly from Kobe the day before, surprising Stephen and Matsu at the house. Ba-Ba appraises Stephen's recovery as Stephen revels in having someone with whom to talk. As they eat dinner and Ba-Ba drinks sake, Stephen confides in his father that he is lonely. Ba-Ba reassures him. Stephen is struck by how close he feels to his father in Tarumi without the distractions of family and business. He wonders if his father has the same feeling, "as if the world were concentrated into just these small rooms" (20).

Autumn: October 6, 1937 Summary

Stephen and his father visit the beach together. Stephen swims and learns that his father is a non-swimmer. In this relaxed atmosphere, Stephen thinks of his father in a new way – almost as an acquaintance – and feels loneliness hovering when he remembers that soon he will return to his business in Kobe.

When Stephen asks about the situation in Shanghai, his father fills him in on the destruction moving south – bombing and fires – and speculates that the Japanese may reach Hong Kong.

Stephen then inquires about Matsu as a younger person; Ba-Ba tells him about how their childhoods intersected in Tarumi when he would visit as a boy. Tomoko, one of Matsu's sisters, was very pretty and caught his eye, but shyness, along with "class and custom" (210), prevented him from pursuing her. Matsu was an energetic young man. He was rumored to be in love with a girl in town who married or moved away. He seemed destined to break away from the village, but when Tomoko died in an accident, Matsu seemed to lose momentum. Stephen imagines that Matsu has a story that remains untold.

Autumn: October 8, 1937 Summary

After saying goodbye to his father at the station, Stephen feels an emptiness. When he returns to the house, Matsu asks him if he'd like to accompany him to see a friend in the nearby mountain village of Yamaguchi, also called the Village of Lepers, due to its history of the diseased traveling there to live in peace. Stephen is surprised at the invitation and quickly agrees. As the two walk uphill to the village, Matsu tells Stephen he used to visit a friend there as a young man and was unafraid of catching leprosy, which a doctor told him could not be contracted by contact.

When they arrive at Yamaguchi, Stephen sees that the houses are made of pieced-together scraps of wood and that the people are mangled by the disease. He recalls the historical Chinese fear of lepers but does not feel fear himself. They arrive at a small, sturdier house; Matsu's step lightens as he approaches and knocks at the door. Matsu's friend Sachi, a woman wearing a black veil to cover the ulcers on the left side of her face, serves them tea. Stephen can see that she was once extraordinarily beautiful and, as they visit, understands that he and Sachi share the experience of solitude.

On the way home, Matsu tells Stephen about leprosy coming to Tarumi forty years ago. It spread quickly, infecting Tarumi's people indiscriminately. They were afraid to let others know of the outbreak since Tarumi was a holiday destination. Matsu shares that leprosy is what killed his sister, Tomoko. Stephen asks, "Why did you take me with you to Yamaguchi?" Matsu answers, "So you would know that you're not alone" (30).

Autumn: October 21, 1937 Summary

Stephen and Matsu's friendship develops. While Matsu remains short on conversation, his demeanor toward Stephen has relaxed, and when Stephen asks when they will visit Yamaguchi and Sachi again, Matsu teases him about his curiosity. Stephen is fascinated by Sachi's mystery and wonders if Matsu and Sachi were or are in love.

Stephen decides to paint the garden view from his grandfather's study. The garden has begun to fascinate him: "Matsu's garden whispers at you, never shouts; it leads you down a path hoping for more, as if everything is seen, yet hidden" (31). He opens the shoji screens and feels happiness and health he hasn't felt in a long time. At first, Matsu seems to object to Stephen's opening up the room, but later, as Stephen paints, Matsu brings him a lunch tray. Next to a bowl of udon is a surprising gift: a lacquer box of sable paintbrushes which belonged to Stephen's grandfather.

Autumn: October 29, 1937 Summary

Absorbed in his painting for several days, Stephen is almost finished with it. He decides to go for a swim while relishing the last touches he will make to the piece. He arrives at the empty beach and removes his shirt; just then, he hears the two girls from before in the distance, then sees them laughing and walking toward him. Partially hidden from their view behind beach grass, Stephen remembers, as the girls come closer, that King told Stephen he intimidated girls at school with his good looks. He stays still so that he won't scare them away and will be able to speak with them.

The younger and shorter of the two girls (a little older than Pie) spots him first, and the older, taller girl with waist-length hair leads the way to greet him. Both girls are a bit shy, but the elder is more confident. Stephen puts his shirt back on and bows hello to them. They giggle and bow back. He introduces himself. Keiko, the older girl, introduces herself and her sister, Mika. After a brief conversation, the girls run back the way they came. Stephen dashes to the water to swim, forgetting to remove his clothes.

Stephen returns to the house and recalls the harmless, childlike spirits he hallucinated at the height of his illness in Hong Kong, and their contrast with the real girls he's just met. He tells Matsu about his beach encounter, and Matsu encourages him by telling him that their resistance is "part of the game" (37). Matsu then gives Stephen the good news that Sachi has invited them to visit the next day.

Autumn: October 5, 1937-Autumn: October 29, 1937 Analysis

In these five chapters, Stephen begins to reckon with his isolation and to learn of life beyond the comforts of his upper-middle-class upbringing. When Ba-Ba visits Tarumi, he tells Stephen about Matsu's sister Tomoko and her death by "some kind of accident" (22), along with Matsu's possible relationship as a youth with a girl who disappeared. There seems to be more to these stories, and a sense of the untold manifests in the narrative.

This sense of the unknown is heightened when Matsu takes Stephen to meet Sachi in Yamaguchi. Stephen finds Sachi beautiful, both in spite of and because of her scars. He is drawn to her. He connects with Yamaguchi's story of transformation into a haven for the suffering. He empathizes with Sachi's story of contracting leprosy and moving there. His psyche expands with his embrace of how the sublime may co-exist with pain: "Her once-beautiful face had even appeared in my dreams, the sadness half-hidden under her black scarf" (31). The scarf is a recurring motif, underlining the idea of the hidden, the secret.

When Stephen begins to paint the garden in his grandfather's study, a number of connections occur: Stephen pays homage Matsu and his work, he makes art in the same space his grandfather used to paint, and he finds himself transforming his isolation into creativity. This painting will emerge as a symbol; it memorializes Stephen's transformation during his time in Tarumi. Like

Stephen's relationship with the girls on the beach, whom he knows now as Keiko and Mika, the painting is coming to life both by Stephen's volition and through its own unfolding: "The garden is a world filled with secrets. Slowly, I see more each day" (31).

Autumn: October 30, 1937-Autumn: November 30, 1937

Autumn: October 30, 1937 Summary

Stephen rises early, excited for the trip to Yamaguchi, to find Matsu in the kitchen making bacon and eggs. This breakfast, uncommon in Japan, reminds Stephen of going to Western hotels for brunch with his parents and siblings. Matsu tells Stephen that his grandfather loved three eggs over-easy and black coffee every morning. The two discuss the beginning of Matsu's long employment with Stephen's grandfather, who died before Stephen really knew him. Matsu describes him as good-looking, smart, and generous, a man who sometimes flaunted his talents but was not offensive. Stephen and Matsu eat together in the kitchen, a new occurrence. Stephen asks if he can bring a gift (he's made a sketch of the ocean) for Sachi. Matsu says it will embarrass her but acquiesces.

When they arrive at Sachi's home in Yamaguchi, she doesn't answer the door. They look for her in her *kare sansui*, a dry garden landscape made of stones that impresses Stephen with its intricacy. Sachi is not there. As they go to look for her, they meet her hurrying up the road from an errand. Inside the house, Stephen gives her his sketch. She is moved by the gift and its subject.

After lunch, Matsu offers to clean up so that Sachi may show Stephen her stone garden. She tells Stephen that

Matsu insisted upon it and helped her to create it when she first came to Yamaguchi. The "beauty and sadness" (43) of the garden make Stephen wonder about Sachi's fate and the role of her family. Later, as Stephen and Matsu walk home, Stephen asks whether she would come visit them if asked. Matsu says it would need to be her choice, that she has not returned in the decades since she left her family in Tarumi in order not to dishonor them with her disease.

Autumn: November 19, 1937 Summary

Upon finishing his painting of Matsu's garden, Stephen feels adrift. He shows his piece to Matsu, who gives it a quick glance and grunts his approval, then asks Stephen if he'd like to go with him into town. Stephen has rarely been into Tarumi before. When the family visited the beach house when Stephen was a child, the servants went into town to get supplies while the family spent time at the beach. The two months he's been at the beach house now have not included a trip into the village.

On the way into town, Matsu and Stephen pass through the train station. Stephen gets some looks not only because of his Chinese appearance, but also because there are not many young men who have not left for military service. The village consists of a store, a post office, a teahouse, and the homes of the villagers. Stephen wonders if he will see Keiko and Mika.

At the teahouse, Matsu introduces Stephen to the owner, Kenzo, a childhood friend who supplies Matsu with bacon and other hard-to-get items. Matsu recalls his first meeting with Kenzo in the garden at the beach house and that Sachi and Tomoko had been popular and great friends. Matsu thinks a great deal of Kenzo and relates that Kenzo should have left the village to make his fortune in the city. Instead, because Kenzo's father was sickly, then died, Kenzo stayed behind to care first for him, and then for his bereaved mother.

Kenzo serves Matsu and Stephen rice crackers and drinks, and the three laugh about the bottled rosewater concoction he gives Stephen – he has been trying to convince patrons to like it for years. When Kenzo shares the news that Japanese troops have captured Soo-chow and nearly Shanghai, Matsu is quick to protect Stephen by changing the subject. Kenzo asks after Sachi, and it pleases him when Matsu gives him a note from her.

Stephen and Matsu leave for the post office; Stephen asks about Kenzo and Sachi. Matsu tells him that they cared for each other when they were young and that Sachi left Kenzo behind when she contracted leprosy. She would not see Kenzo, only Matsu: "it was easier for Sachi to see someone she didn't care for" (49). At the post office, Matsu goes to his box and brings back an envelope he hands to Stephen. It has Stephen's name on it.

Autumn: November 20, 1937 Summary

Stephen writes that the morning is heavy and gray, portending a big storm. Stephen reads and re-reads the letter he's received from his mother: his father is keeping a woman in Kobe, and Mah-mee wants to know if Stephen has known anything about the affair. She has always known that her husband might seek companionship, living far away from his family; she has said nothing as he has remained a good provider. However, she has learned from the family banker that Stephen's father has been withdrawing large sums of money in a woman's name and has asked to borrow against the Hong Kong house. She suggests that Stephen is old enough to understand and might return to Kobe to learn what is happening. Stephen empathizes with her embarrassment and loss, but he does not share her sense of his maturity and does want to leave Tarumi yet.

As Stephen attempts to write back to his mother, the storm hits. He and Matsu hurry to slide heavy boards over the house's shoji panels to protect the structure from the heavy wind and rain. As the storm grows stronger, the ocean rages closer, over the beach and toward the house. Waves begin crashing over the property. One of them slams Stephen hard into the house.

Autumn: November 24, 1938 Summary

Stephen awakes in bed, a nasty bump behind his ear and his head pounding. The shoji are still sealed by the boards; he doesn't know if it's day or night. Getting his bearings, he remembers blacking out from impact. He hears voices, and Matsu enters, a bandage on his cheek, followed by Sachi. Concerned for her friends in the storm, she has come from Yamaguchi for the first time in forty years. Wondering if she will stay or go, Stephen begins to lose consciousness. He hears Matsu and Sachi discussing a doctor as he fades out.

Later, Stephen awakes to bright light. He dresses and goes to the garden, which has been destroyed by the storm. He finds Matsu working there and learns that he has been down for two days. He wonders if Sachi's appearance was a hallucination, but she emerges from behind the house: she has come for the second time to check on him. Stephen asks if he can help with the garden. At first, Matsu refuses. Sachi reminds him that he once told her that working in a garden would return her to life. "Only light work then, until you're better" (56), says Matsu.

Autumn: November 30, 1937 Summary

Sachi begins coming to the house very early every day to help Matsu and Stephen with the garden, leaving again at twilight. Sachi and Stephen's friendship grows as the garden takes its shape again. Stephen writes a brief letter to his mother letting her know that he must recover from the storm; he dreads speaking to his father.

One day as they work, Stephen asks Sachi about her return, which feels to her like a dream. She's been given courage by her will to help Matsu and Stephen. When Stephen brings up Kenzo, Sachi says that he was a hard friend to lose, but she has always had Matsu and has made friends in Yamaguchi. She points to Matsu's rebuilt bridge and tells Stephen that Matsu once told her it represented the samurai's brave journey to the afterlife. Standing at the top of the bridge, one can see paradise; this is how she feels, living newly without fear. As they replant a pine together, Sachi tells Stephen that soon the garden will look just like his painting again. He is surprised that Matsu has shown her the painting, since he said nothing when Stephen showed it to him. Sachi says, "everything is in what he does not say" (58).

Stephen comes to see Sachi's scars, which he glimpses sometimes, as beautiful. He enjoys Matsu and Sachi's sweet friendship and wonders about futures past in which they or Sachi and Kenzo might have been married. The happiness and nostalgia of the present are interrupted when the radio announces that Shanghai has been occupied.

The same evening, Stephen hears Keiko and Mika at the gate. When he opens it, Keiko is there alone. She tells him that they heard he wasn't well and hands him a gift: a black lacquer box wrapped in maroon cloth. Inside are *yokan*: red bean cakes. Stephen asks her in, but she says she cannot stay. He asks if he will see her again, and when she demures, he asks if they can set a time. She suggests ten the next morning at the beach.

Stephen is in bed when Matsu comes home from walking Sachi back to Yamaguchi. Stephen offers Matsu some of Keiko's red bean cakes. He tells Matsu about his date tomorrow, and Matsu teases him affectionately. Stephen asks whether Sachi has ever made Matsu yokan; Matsu responds that Stephen should be asking if Matsu has made it for her. Matsu then says he has not, adding that Sachi would have given it back if he did.

Autumn: October 30, 1937-Autumn: November 30, 1937 Analysis

These five chapters span a month. Stephen and Matsu visit Sachi again, and she shows Stephen her stone garden, a wonder that is both literally and figuratively transformative. Its miniature topography may be groomed into different patterns, and Sachi's work there has changed her as a person, empowering her in the wake of her disease. The garden is a symbol of duality – solid and fluid, stark and lovely, before and after: "Her garden was a mixture of beauty and sadness, the rocks and stones an illusion of movement" (43).

Matsu introduces Stephen to his old friend Kenzo at the teahouse in Tarumi, and Stephen begins to learn of Kenzo's relationship with Sachi: how he loved then abandoned her, and how her disease dishonored her family. There are many details still to come, but it is clear that love, honor, and abandonment run deep in this triangle of old friends.

Stephen stands out in the village, both because he is Chinese and because most of the young Japanese men have gone off to war. A theme – the individual vs. the collective – begins to emerge: in theory, and in the news, the Chinese hate the Japanese and vice-versa. They are at war. Yet in reality, Stephen and several others in the novel have strong, empathetic relationships that cross cultural boundaries. We see that cultural and political affiliation may be far less powerful, over time, than basic human needs like love and comfort.

When Stephen's mother writes to Stephen of his father's infidelity, a storm hits. The symbol of weather is again evident: Stephen's turmoil at his mother's revelations is reflected in the pelting wind and rain and the encroaching waves: "It seemed like the storm would last forever, as it steadily grew in strength. The wind and rain continued, and the noise of the violent sea was deafening" (52). The garden is destroyed by a wall of water from the sea, and Stephen is knocked out by the wave, which symbolizes the force of his emotions.

When Sachi comes down from Yamaguchi to help Matsu and Stephen rebuild the garden, the redemptive quality of friendship is clear, and Stephen's connections with Sachi and Matsu deepen. Stephen also connects further with Keiko when she brings him *yokan* after his injury. The motif of food is again grounding; Keiko's gift, like Sachi's presence, shows kindness and hope in the face of disaster.

Autumn: December 1, 1937-Winter: December 7, 1937

Autumn: December 1, 1937 Summary

Stephen leaves Matsu and Sachi working together happily in the much-improved garden and goes to the calm, storm-littered beach to meet Keiko. She arrives alone, having won a bet to get Mika to stay home doing laundry. They walk and talk. Keiko is curious about life in Hong Kong, and she tells Stephen about growing up in Tarumi and that she has a brother who was born near Kobe and is now in the Japanese army in China.

Stephen walks Keiko halfway back to the village, where she stops him: her traditionalist father might not approve of their visit. They part sweetly, with the idea of seeing each other again, and Stephen returns to the beach house. There, he hears three voices, one angry, from inside. Stephen doesn't go in; he watches, unseen.

Kenzo is there. He is enraged that Sachi has been visiting Matsu. He shoves Matsu, who doesn't retaliate. But when he yanks the scarf from Sachi's face and calls her a monster, Matsu shoves him out the back door, sending him tumbling down the stairs. Sachi cries out. Stephen remains hidden, afraid of doubling her shame. When Matsu takes Sachi back to Yamaguchi, Stephen doubts she will return to Tarumi.

Autumn: December 2, 1937 Summary

Matsu tells Stephen that there was trouble the day before, explaining that Kenzo brought a letter for Matsu to deliver to Sachi in Yamaguchi. Kenzo was shocked to see her. She invited him in for tea. Stephen admits that he knows about the scuffle. Matsu explains that Kenzo and Sachi were once engaged and that he was and has been their go-between; Kenzo's shame at abandoning her when she became ill was too great, and he never visited her. Matsu has never admitted his feelings for Sachi to Kenzo. Matsu says that Sachi will never return. Stephen offers to speak with her. "I will not have Sachi hurt anymore" (70), says Matsu.

Winter: December 5, 1937 Summary

Stephen tries to paint. Matsu works in the garden. Both feel the emptiness left by Sachi's departure. Stephen decides to visit Sachi in secret; he wakes before Matsu and leaves a note, saying he has gone for a walk.

When Stephen arrives at Sachi's house, she is happy to see him. He lies, saying that he is concerned that she might be ill. She invites him in and brings tea. She tells Stephen that her presence in Tarumi has dishonored everyone, that Kenzo is convinced that she and Matsu have been deceiving him for many years. Impulsively, Stephen touches Sachi's scars. He tells her that Matsu needs her. She responds by exposing her whole face, which is more scarred than Stephen realized: "Does Matsu need this?" (76), Sachi asks. Stephen finds her even more beautiful than before and answers yes.

Sachi leads Stephen to her garden. She works on the stones, changing their patterns, her face uncovered. Stephen thinks of Mah-mee, feels her pain, and resolves to write to her when he returns to Tarumi. He begins working on the stones with Sachi. Referring to Matsu's idea that she make the garden, Sachi says that she had always thought it would be Kenzo, not Matsu, who saved her. But, she reveals, when Tomoko took her life by seppuku because her great beauty was threatened by leprosy, Matsu's kind, respectful silence – rather than Kenzo's more outgoing, popular personality – helped Sachi to recover from her friend's death. They became friends, and Matsu gave her Tomoko's lucky stones after the funeral. Matsu did, in fact, have dreams of moving away from Tarumi, but because of Sachi, he never left.

Stephen admits he has lied to Matsu about visiting Sachi. She tells him that he may visit again, with Matsu's knowledge.

Winter: December 6, 1937 Summary

Matsu is working in the garden when Stephen arrives. Stephen confesses to his trip to see Sachi. Matsu is pleased that she is all right. He informs Stephen that his father has come.

Stephen's father is waiting in the study, which has become Stephen's painting studio. His business suit and fedora seem out of place among the painting supplies. He is pleased with Stephen's health and his artistic progress. He tells Stephen that he knows about his mother's letter and that a Japanese woman would never do such a thing. Stephen snaps back that perhaps a Japanese woman would not be so aware of what her husband was doing.

Stephen's father reveals that he has been seeing a woman, Yoshiko, for twelve years and that Stephen's mother was never to have known, but that with the war, money has become tight. Stephen is shocked: this is a long-term affair, not a fling. Stephen's father assures him that he loves them all, and that he is here not to apologize but to explain that he has always weighed his decisions carefully. He says that there will be no divorce, that nothing will change. For Stephen, his father's integrity has eroded.

Winter: December 7, 1937 Summary

Stephen and his father discuss the war. The troops are moving toward Canton. Stephen considers his father's dual life in Japan and China and knows that when his father must choose, his choice will be China. Stephen juxtaposes his own relationships with Matsu and Sachi against the savagery of the Japanese army. He wonders if he must soon return to Hong Kong. His father invites him to Kobe for the holidays; Stephen is noncommittal.

When Stephen wakes the next morning, his father has already left for Kobe. He feels that he has failed both of his parents: he has not been able to accept his father's mistress as his father wishes, and he has not convinced his father to leave Yoshiko for his mother.

Matsu asks if Stephen would like to visit Tama, a Shinto shrine, later in the day. Stephen's family is not religious; he attended Catholic school when younger but doesn't identify strongly with any belief. Stephen says yes and begins a letter to Mah-mee.

The letter focuses on Stephen's father's visit and the upcoming holidays. He tells his mother that his father's bank account withdrawals were to help a friend with her business. He hates the lie and having to tell it. He asks after Pie.

As Matsu and Stephen walk through town toward the mountain shrine, they pass Kenzo's teahouse tensely. No one emerges. At the shrine, they move through three red *torii* gates and purify themselves with water before entering. Inside the shrine, surrounded by incense smoke and prayers written on white slips of paper, is a stone table with a wooden box containing the fox deity Inari. Matsu prays and makes an offering. He shows Stephen how to pray, clapping three times and pulling on a rope. Stephen does not know whom or what to pray for, so he prays simply for "all of us" (90).

Stephen and Matsu eat lunch outdoors. Matsu admits that he thought the shrine visit would be good for Stephen. Upset, Stephen asks if Matsu knew about his father's affair. Matsu says that he does not concern himself with Stephen's father's private life. Stephen snaps at Matsu, then apologizes. Matsu says he knows that it was "the anger speaking, not the man," that Stephen's new knowledge doesn't change how his father feels about him, and that it is "sad to think that sometimes one person's happiness must come at the expense of others" (91).

Stephen asks if Matsu came to pray for Kenzo, and Matsu says no, that their friendship will have to rely on its history. Stephen thinks of his parents and wonders if he might be able to change the future for them.

Autumn: December 1, 1937-Winter: December 7, 1937 Analysis

In these chapters, Stephen gets to know Tarumi and its people on a deeper level. One day, he returns from a meeting with Keiko during which they discuss her brother's having joined the Japanese army (a possible source of discord between Keiko's family and a Chinese suitor) to find Matsu, Sachi, and Kenzo in conflict at the beach house. Kenzo has discovered Sachi there and is enraged at what he perceives as a betrayal. He calls Sachi a "monster" (67), and a physical fight ensues between the two men.

Stephen hides during the altercation but admits that he was present in a subsequent visit to Sachi in Yamaguchi. Sachi is horrified by the fight: "My presence there has brought great dishonor to all of you" (75). She reveals more details about Tomoko's disease and suicide to Stephen and shows him two special stones Tomoko gave her long ago that are supposed to bring good luck. These stones will become a symbol of hope; they are passed down from innocent Tomoko and Sachi through life-worn, older Sachi (later) to Stephen as he makes his own journey from innocence to experience.

Stephen's father makes a surprise visit to the beach house. He explains but does not show remorse for his affair. Stephen defends his mother but realizes that nothing will change as his father describes how he has lived and will live his life: "I'm not here to apologize to you, Stephen. This has never been a simple matter for me. I have spent my life doing what I thought was the right thing to do" (84).

In contrast, transparency grows between Stephen and Matsu. Stephen tells Matsu that he witnessed the fight with Kenzo, and Matsu takes Stephen to the Tama shrine in Tarumi. There, Matsu shows Stephen how to perform the proper rituals. Stephen sees, near the altar, a physical manifestation of the hopes and fears of those around him: "…hundreds of small white slips of paper. Matsu whispered that they contained prayers and offerings from the villagers" (89).

This symbol of transcendence, the prayer slips, will return later in the novel. The image provides a sense of secrecy and desire (the folded paper and enclosed writing) and becomes more than mere description as it is tied to the importance of writing in Stephen's own life, his own fears, and his hope that he will transcend conflict and isolation to find peace and love.

The theme of solitude and connection and the theme of the individual vs. the collective appear again in these chapters: Stephen feels his own solitude and that of those around him, yet is connected to them by acts of kindness. Even as his friendship with Keiko grows, he faces possible rejection by Keiko's family because of his nationality.

Winter: December 21, 1937-Winter: February 4, 1938

Winter: December 21, 1937 Summary

For two weeks, Stephen has avoided thinking of his parents. A letter arrives from his mother.

She says that Stephen's father has told her the same thing Stephen wrote about helping a friend in business and that she must accept this explanation, having married Stephen's father when she was only fifteen and having no way to make a living on her own now, at forty. She also accepts that she and Stephen's father may need to share family and finances but live separate lives. She notes that she had hoped to join Stephen in Tarumi for the holidays but will stay in Hong Kong because of her health. She suggests that he go to Kobe and expresses concern about his recovery.

Stephen remembers his younger years, before Pie was born and business took his father to Japan more and more often, when his parents were close and the family spent happy evenings together in Hong Kong. He feels the family's changes and his own changes acutely. He wires his father to tell him that he will stay in Tarumi for the holidays.

Winter: December 25, 1937 Summary

Stephen wakes to his first Christmas morning in Tarumi. Matsu has made a Christmas tree for him in the garden, decorating it with origami cranes and fish. Stephen remembers his Christmases growing up in Hong Kong, the ornate Western-style tree, the children waiting for their parents to rise to open presents, five-course Christmas dinners at the Hong Kong Hotel with lectures from Mahmee on how to use the formal Western silverware. He considers Matsu's tree: "it's the nicest Christmas tree I've ever had" (94), he says sincerely.

Winter: January 1, 1938 Summary

Ganjitsu, New Year's Day, is a national festival for the Japanese. Stephen finds it to be much unlike Chinese New Year – spiritual as opposed to boisterous, with simple gifts, debts repaid, and visits to holy places. Stephen is thrilled to learn that he and Matsu will be celebrating with Sachi.

Matsu has been preparing for days, making special dishes and *kado-matsu*, holiday wreaths. Stephen has purchased a tiny pine tree for Sachi, and Matsu and Stephen have exchanged gifts: a good-luck *daruma* doll for Matsu (it is tradition to make wishes, then draw in eyes as the wishes come true) and a book of Japanese poetry for Stephen.

As they leave for Yamaguchi, Stephen asks Matsu what the *kado-matsu* symbolize. "[P]rosperity, purity, longevity, and loyalty" (96), says Matsu. Matsu tells him that he has made a wreath for Sachi and another for Kenzo. When Stephen and Matsu arrive in Yamaguchi, the village is celebrating. Sachi's house is quiet, but she is dressed festively and excited to see them. Stephen thinks of the fresh starts the new year will bring for everyone.

Winter: January 15, 1938 Summary

Stephen has received gifts from his family and a letter from King, who is home for the holidays in Hong Kong. At first, the letter takes Stephen back fondly to his time at school, but it turns to disturbing news of the thousands of Chinese raped and murdered in the Nanking Massacre. King says he would join the fight if he thought China could win but will instead return to Canton against his family's wishes, promising to come home if the Japanese get too close.

Winter: February 4, 1938 Summary

The First Rites of Spring, or Setsubun, takes Matsu and Stephen to the Tama Shrine. A crowd is there for *mame-maki*, a bean-throwing ritual performed by the monks that heralds new life in spring. Stephen looks for Keiko; Matsu seems to be looking for Kenzo.

Though Stephen has gained strength during his time in Tarumi, he still tires easily. On the way home, he and Matsu pause near Kenzo's teahouse. A crowd has gathered. Many notice Matsu and speak in hushed whispers. Matsu and Stephen push their way into the teahouse to find Kenzo's body hanging from the rafters.

Matsu lowers his friend's body to a counter, allowing no one else to touch it. He stands silently with Kenzo, then whispers in his ear, carefully closes his eyelids, and walks slowly home.

Winter: December 21, 1937-Winter: February 4, 1938 Analysis

While these five chapters are shorter than many others, they pack a great deal into a few pages. The holidays have arrived, and Stephen is pleased with the delightful simplicity of the Japanese celebrations, compared to the more boisterous, Westernized ones of his childhood in China. Sachi, Matsu, and Stephen celebrate together and exchange gifts. Winter is symbolic of death; as the village celebrates a new year, the old one passes.

The letter from King is unsettling: he writes from Canton about the Nanking Massacre, thousands of Chinese people raped and murdered by the Japanese. The news stands in stark contrast to the peaceful, spiritual moments Stephen is experiencing with his Tarumi friends. Again we see the theme of the individual vs. the collective: War is sweeping across the larger world, yet individual relationships carry on, growing and changing.

The theme of suicide hits home in the present as this group of chapters comes to a close: As Stephen and Matsu leave a celebration of spring in town, they find that Kenzo has hung himself in the teahouse. Before, suicide had been something that happened in the distant past in this circle of friends. Now, it is immediate, visceral: "Matsu lowered Kenzo's body from the wooden beam. He wouldn't allow anyone else to touch his friend. I could hear the low thud of Kenzo's body as it fell to the counter...." (99). In this new year, traditionally a time of forgiveness, hope, and change, Kenzo – deeply conflicted about his love and abandonment of Sachi and her relationship with Matsu – has chosen to leave this life. The symbol of winter deepens.

Before, we have heard characters' remembrances of the past in the present. Now, the idea of present and past becomes a theme: they are not separate, one real and one conceptual. One overlays the other, and they affect each other with deep emotional resonance and real consequences.

Winter: February 5, 1938- Winter: March 14, 1938

Winter: February 5, 1938 Summary

Stephen is left breathless and nauseated by the shock of Kenzo's death. He stumbles home with Matsu, vomits, and needs Matsu's assistance to get to bed. Stephen passes in and out of sleep as Matsu drinks whiskey and listens to the radio, which blares news of Japanese progress toward Canton. Stephen knows that their next stop will be Hong Kong and wonders if he should go home to his mother and sister or join his father in Kobe.

When Stephen rises, Matsu is gone. He doesn't return until much later, when he silently makes the evening meal.

Winter: February 6, 1938 Summary

Matsu informs Stephen that Kenzo will be buried the next morning in a Buddhist ceremony. Other than this, Matsu has been eerily silent. "Since I'd arrived in Tarumi, Matsu had been the anchor and I was the one afloat. I wasn't ready to switch places" (102), writes Stephen. Matsu tells Stephen that yesterday, he went to tell Sachi of Kenzo's suicide.

Matsu tells Stephen that strangely, at the news of Kenzo's death, Sachi began speaking about a Tama Matsuri festival many years ago during which Matsu rescued her from being crushed by a frenzied crowd while popular Kenzo helped carry the festival shrine. Matsu had long thought that this rescue had been anonymous; it turns out that Sachi has guessed that it was him all along, even though Tomoko spread the rumor that Kenzo was the rescuer. Sachi apologizes to Matsu: "Sometimes you can't see what is right in front of you" (104). Matsu reflects on the fact that both he and Kenzo were faithful to Sachi for decades: while Kenzo couldn't accept Sachi's changed appearance and Matsu visited her faithfully, neither man found himself able to leave Tarumi or be with another woman. Sachi comments on all of their suffering and says she will not attend Kenzo's funeral.

Stephen writes to his mother, focusing on the pleasant holidays and avoiding news of his father and Kenzo. Feeling physically better, he goes to the post office to drop off the letter and pick up the mail for Matsu. After his errand, he feels someone tap his arm and turns to see Keiko, carrying a basket of persimmons.

They exchange greetings, and Keiko asks why Kenzo would take his own life. Stephen says only that the suicide is sad. He offers to carry Keiko's basket home for her. She agrees, then changes her mind. As they both pull on the basket, the persimmons tumble out. Keiko seems frantic about her father seeing her with Stephen; Stephen does not know if this is because her father is old-fashioned or because Stephen is Chinese. Keiko collects the persimmons and hurries away.

Winter: February 7, 1938 Summary

The village gathers for Kenzo's burial. Stephen, wearing an ill-fitting dark kimono and wooden sandals borrowed from Matsu for the event, sees that he is the only young man there – all of the other young men have moved away or joined the Japanese army. He feels like a fish out of water. The crowd moves in procession to the Buddhist temple.

During the incense-thick ceremony, Stephen sees Keiko, Mika, and their parents. Afterward, he approaches them; Keiko's father looks at him with a glare so full of hate that Stephen ducks his head and walks away. As he leaves the temple, he sees a black-veiled figure hovering nearby, among the trees. It is Sachi. They bow to one another, and when Stephen looks up, she is gone.

Winter: March 7, 1938 Summary

Since the funeral, life seems frozen. There is no news from Stephen's family, and both Sachi and Keiko have disappeared. Stephen sleeps late and does little. Matsu has stayed close to the house and away from Yamaguchi. Stephen has not told him of Sachi's presence at the shrine.

Winter: March 14, 1938 Summary

Matsu goes into town, and Stephen, feeling restless, sketches in the garden. He hears footsteps, then a knock at the gate: It is Keiko. She apologizes for her father's behavior, saying that even though her brother is fighting in the war against Stephen's nation, her father should not have been rude to Stephen. Stephen invites her into the garden but she refuses. Before she can refuse again, he offers to walk her home, then joins her outside the gate.

Stephen and Keiko walk down the beach. She explains that she has had to lie to get away from Mika and her father in order to see him. They pause on the sand, and Stephen kisses her. Keiko says she must leave but promises she will come again. Stephen writes, "I didn't want her to leave so soon, still feeling the warm rush of desire. But I stood there, my feet pressing deep imprints into the sand" (114).

Winter: February 5, 1938- Winter: March 14, 1938 Analysis

These chapters occur in the wake of Kenzo's suicide. Stephen is reeling, shocked to the point of nausea. He hears on the radio that the Japanese are nearing Canton and wonders, all things considered, if he should return home. Matsu recounts his own visit to Sachi in Yamaguchi to tell her of Kenzo's death and relates an old story Sachi told him from her perspective during the visit that makes clear the different kinds of loyalty Matsu and Kenzo have showed her over the years. When Matsu tells her that Kenzo didn't suffer, she says, "'But haven't we all been suffering for years?'" (105).

Stephen sees Keiko three times – first a sweet but nervous hello when he is leaving the post office on an errand, then at Kenzo's funeral, then in the garden. At the funeral, Stephen encounters Keiko's whole family. Her father is offended by Stephen's presence and snubs him angrily with "a look so full of hate I simply bowed my head and walked quickly away" (110). Keiko later comes to the garden to apologize to Stephen. They walk on the beach, and Stephen's desire for her grows.

All themes develop in this chapter: suicide is front and center, rippling through Tarumi; Stephen feels both isolated from and connected to Keiko, in a manner similar to how Kenzo and Matsu were with Sachi; in Stephen's interaction with Keiko's father, we see that her father perceives Stephen as part of a collective, not as an individual: the more we learn about the past, the more we understand the present.

Imagery and motif continue to support plot and character. For example, the persimmons Keiko carries in a basket during her meeting with Stephen at the post office operate much as the flowers associated with her before – they show grace, and also abundance. Her spilling of them in her nervousness shows the conflict between her feelings for Stephen and her sense of familial obligation. Stephen tries to calm her, putting her feelings before his own: "I paused, but seeing her anxiousness I placed the persimmons back into the basket without another word" (108).

Spring: March 28, 1938-Spring: May 30, 1938

Spring: March 28, 1938 Summary

The changing season and the memory of Keiko's kiss have brought warmth and lightness to both the garden and Stephen's psyche. He returns from a swim to a letter from Pie, who explains that she hasn't written for some time due to volunteering at the Red Cross refugee center in Wan Chai, where refugees are crowded into shantytowns, suffering hunger and heavy rains. She begs Stephen not to tell their mother, who has been in a bad mood, absorbed in her mah-jongg and charities. Mah-mee would be horrified that Pie, who she assumes is at an Errol Flynn movie or shopping, is mixing with the poor refugees.

Pie closes with her and her mother's fear that Stephen may not be safe in Japan and their hope that he will be home soon. Stephen wishes he could tell Pie that he feels safe with Matsu and Sachi, and that he is just coming to know Keiko.

Spring: April 15, 1938 Summary

Stephen decides to visit Sachi, but he gets out of bed to find Matsu gone. The radio informs him that there has been a setback for the Japanese – the Chinese have prevailed in the battle of Taierchwang. Stephen celebrates by beginning a painting in the study. Matsu returns and, instead of staying quiet as usual, expresses happiness that Stephen is working, then tells him – a happy synchronicity for Stephen – that they will visit Sachi today.

As Matsu and Stephen near Yamaguchi, they smell something burning. They run to the village, where a fire spreads wildly. In the confusion and thick smoke, Stephen helps Hiro, a fingerless villager, throw seemingly futile buckets of water on the leaping flames. Matsu digs fire breaks.

Hours later, the fire is out. Only a few houses have been destroyed. Sachi and her home are intact. Matsu praises Stephen and tells him that his grandfather also would be proud. Even after breathing the ashy air, Stephen has never felt healthier. He feels for the villagers, their solitude allowing them no Red Cross, their encroaching age making them vulnerable. Sachi approaches the men and bows low, expressing her gratitude.

Inside Sachi's house, the trio have tea. Matsu and Stephen learn that the fire started from a pile of magazines. Sachi juxtaposes her friends' actions against the villagers' – the villagers had everything to lose, but Matsu and Stephen risked their lives in sheer bravery. Matsu corrects her: "We had more to lose than you could know" (123). Sachi blushes. Stephen leaves so that Sachi and Matsu can be alone.

Matsu and Stephen decide to stay the night with Hiro in Yamaguchi. Hiro tells Stephen that long ago, Matsu helped the villagers to construct their humble homes, assisting them by carrying materials from Tarumi, and that Matsu cannot be taken at "face value." Stephen jokes that none of the villagers can. Hiro asks what Stephen's perfect face can tell them. "That I have a lot to learn" (124), answers Stephen.

Very early the next morning, Stephen visits Sachi's stone garden. As he stands there in the dawn light, he fears that his time in Japan is growing short. He does not think Sachi will be awake, but she enters, surprising him, wanting to show him something: a small cluster of purple balloon flowers growing among the rocks. She explains that for a long time, she could not bear to see flowers as they reminded her of the past and its unattainable beauty, but that now she is grateful for them and their hopeful message. Their conversation touches on the war and Kenzo's death; Stephen tells Sachi that he has not told Matsu about her presence at the funeral. She bows to him.

Stephen asks Sachi for more about her past. They pause for lunch, then Sachi dives farther back into her story and her deeper truth: She recounts meeting Matsu (so quiet she assumed he didn't like her) and Tomoko (beautiful and ambitious) as children, her blossoming friendship with Tomoko, and becoming betrothed to Kenzo. She shares her discovery of her own illness via a rash on her arm a year after Tomoko's death and that she confided in Matsu, who arranged for her to see a doctor. She tells Stephen that when the rash spread, she finally admitted to Kenzo that she had leprosy, and he walked out on her.

Sachi says that when the disease began to spread faster in Tarumi, she and four other afflicted made a plan to commit seppuku in the sea, to prevent bringing shame to their families. Only Sachi was unable to follow through with the act. She ran to the woods and hid, hungry and cold. Matsu found her, assured her that her family believed that she had died, and told her, "It takes greater courage to live" (139). He knew of Yamaguchi, a haven for villagers and others from farther away who would or could not commit suicide, for it was where he had hoped to bring Tomoko.

Matsu brought Sachi to Yamaguchi. It was still an undeveloped village – dirty, ramshackle, and full of the stench and sight of rotting appendages. Sachi tried to flee, but Matsu took her to the home of Michiko, an old woman ravaged by the disease, who convinced her to stay with her

39

kind care. Sachi, used to being treated like royalty in Tarumi, had a tortured adjustment to Yamaguchi. Matsu's frequent presence as he assisted in the village soothed her. Then, for days, he did not come.

To calm Sachi in Matsu's absence, Michiko told her a story about a girl named Sumiko who wanted nothing more than to become a pearl diver. When she did, it was everything she had dreamed and more. She married a boy named Akio, and soon they were joyfully pregnant. But to protect the baby, Sumiko had to stop pearl diving. Her spirit failed as her belly grew, and Akio feared for her life. He took her to the water, where she swam away. Three months later, she returned, the baby in her arms. She gave the child, Kuniko, to Akio and returned to the sea. Years later, when Kuniko told Akio that she wished to become a pearl diver, he did not stop her. He knew that her mother would always be there to protect her.

When Matsu returned the next day, having been ill, he told Sachi that Michiko had once been a pearl diver and that she had had a child. Sachi found herself changed, humbled, empathizing with the lives around her. Years passed, and the village took shape. With Matsu's help, Sachi began working in the village gardens, then building a house, then creating her own stone garden. She learned about beauty – the physical kind that fades and the deeper kind that persists. As Michiko neared death, Sachi cared for her. She was comforted that Michiko would once again dive for pearls, reunited with her daughter Kuniko.

When Sachi was in her early twenties, Kenzo figured out that she was alive. Kenzo began to send her food and messages, reigniting her sense of loss. During a short time when Matsu was unable to visit, Sachi again raged against the trap of her life, considering suicide. A strong wind sent her barefoot into the stone garden, where her perspective changed once and for all: "its beauty was one that no disease or person could ever take away from me. I stood there for a long time until I felt like I was no longer myself at all, but part of the garden" (152).

As Sachi finishes her story, in present day, Matsu enters the house.

Spring: April 22, 1938 Summary

Matsu is pleased that Stephen has visited Sachi. The two men return to Tarumi to collect supplies for fixing the burned houses in Yamaguchi. Stephen feels a bit worn down, and Matsu notices; living together a while now, they've begun to "read each other's minds" (154).

Matsu tells Stephen more about Tomoko, how she became more serious and less a flighty young girl as her disease progressed. One night, she asked Matsu to help her find their father's fishing knife so that she could end her life. Matsu refused. A few days later, Tomoko found the knife and took matters into her own hands.

Spring: May 15, 1938 Summary

Stephen and Matsu have made several supply deliveries to Yamaguchi and are ready to begin building. On this morning, Stephen stays home to rest. He becomes restless and listens to Matsu's radio: The Japanese have taken Hsuchowfu, an important railway junction between Nanking and Peking. Stephen knows that Canton and Hong Kong may be next. Stephen writes letters to Pie and Mah-mee, saying that he will return home.

Matsu returns, and Stephen is ready to tell him about his decision. Matsu hands Stephen a letter from Mah-mee. She urges Stephen to stay in Tarumi for his health, reminds him that Hong Kong may stay safe because it is under British rule, and says that she and Pie will not visit him because things are still in flux between her and Ba-Ba. She mentions an uncle named Sing, a friend of Ba-Ba's, with whom she has been spending time; Stephen does not remember him. Sing was ill as a young man, too, and has assured Mah-mee that Stephen will recover.

Stephen goes to the garden and finds Matsu there sharpening his father's fishing knife.

Spring: May 30, 1938 Summary

Stephen and Matsu are the guests of honor at a celebration for the homes they've rebuilt in Yamaguchi. Stephen calls it "one of the best nights of my life" (160). Later that night, Stephen has a sake-induced dream that Yamaguchi is in Hong Kong and that Pie is there, tending to Hiro and the other villagers.

Spring: March 28, 1938-Spring: May 30, 1938 Analysis

As these five chapters open, spring arrives. The weather changes with the season, and spring symbolizes newness and rebirth. Stephen is hopeful about his new relationship with Keiko: "it has been much warmer the past few weeks. Since the day I saw Keiko, I've felt much lighter. It's as if the darkness of winter has lifted" (116). He also receives hopeful news from Pie: as the war continues, she has begun serving refugees in Hong Kong; service works with the theme of isolation and connection, showing how people may connect through empathy.

When fire threatens Yamaguchi, Stephen and Matsu help the villagers to save it from destruction. Sachi tells Stephen the story of her own rebirth when her leprosy spread, Kenzo rejected her, she tried and failed to commit seppuku, and Matsu took her to Yamaguchi, where she grew from an entitled and broken girl into a self-aware woman working with others to build a future. She formed a relationship with Michiko, a caring older woman who had once been a pearl diver; with Matsu's help, she created the stone garden. She learned that beauty dwells within: "If I hadn't learned humility before then, from that day on I knew what the word meant. Here in Yamaguchi I learned that beauty exists where you least expect to find it" (148). The theme of solitude and connection is the core of Yamaguchi and its suffering, redeemed souls. She also learned about real friendship – while Kenzo learned of her survival and began to send gifts of tinned food, Matsu stood by her, becoming her life companion. The "balloon flowers" (137) that appear in the stone garden, continuing the flower motif, remind her of life's blessings and bring her back to the present and Stephen: "...the good fortune to find a new friend such as you" (127).

This group of chapters closes with Matsu's memories of Tomoko's suicide, then a celebration of Yamaguchi's rebirth. Stephen dreams of Pie serving the villagers, creating connection across personal and national borders.

Summer: June 6, 1938-Summer: July 5, 1938

Summer: June 6, 1938 Summary

The brightness of summer brings Stephen to Tarumi with Matsu for the first time since Kenzo's funeral. The teahouse remains closed. Stephen has learned that Ba-Ba will visit; Stephen mails letters to his mother and Pie letting them know that he is fine. Leaving the post office, he sees Keiko coming confidently toward him. She tells him that she feared he might have returned to Hong Kong and asks him to meet her the next day at the Tama shrine. She touches his hand gently before walking away.

When Matsu and Stephen return home, Sachi is there. She informs them that Hiro has passed away in his sleep. Matsu returns to Yamaguchi with Sachi, leaving Stephen to rest. Stephen feels "growing pains," deaths and endings, "the dull ache of being pulled in other directions" (165).

Summer: June 7, 1938 Summary

Matsu has not returned from Yamaguchi overnight. Stephen meets Keiko at the shrine. She has brought a *furoshiki* packed with food and tea. They share the refreshments, then Stephen reclines. He notices Keiko's "scent of jasmine" (166) very close. They kiss, then make love. Stephen wakes to find it's been a dream. Keiko tells Stephen that she dreads the tourists who will soon descend on Tarumi and that she wishes to study architecture at university. Stephen longs to hold her hand as they leave the shrine.

Back at the beach house, Matsu has returned. He tells Stephen that Hiro has been buried. In Matsu, Yamaguchi's "unlikely hero," Stephen sees "cracks in his armor, grief in the curve of his back" (167).

Summer: June 15, 1938 Summary

Stephen's father has come and gone. They avoided the topic of Stephen's mother, focusing on weather and the war. Stephen noticed that even though his father refers to the Japanese as "they," he behaves in a more Japanese than

Chinese manner. Ba-Ba informed Stephen that he and Mah-mee have agreed that Stephen should stay in Tarumi until fall. Ba-Ba offers Stephen the chance to visit him in Kobe for a festival; Stephen lies and says that he has heard of one he'd like to attend at the same time in Tarumi.

Summer: June 29, 1938 Summary

The six-week Baiu (plum rains) have begun. Stephen sees Matsu in the misty garden. On canvas, he is unable to capture the "ghostly beauty" (170) of his friend emerging from the mist.

Summer: July 5, 1938 Summary

Stephen has been swimming in the mist and rain. Recently, in the village, he's seen Mika and Keiko. There is something intimate between Stephen and Keiko now – even though Keiko could not greet him, they share a sweet moment.

Summer: June 6, 1938-Summer: July 5, 1938 Analysis

The season changes again in these chapters. They, along with the next five chapters, serve as a sort of punctuation between the longer, more psychologically complex sections of the novel.

Hiro, a core member of Tarumi, dies, the old giving way to the new. Summer symbolizes fruition, and the plum rains bring emotional and physical union for Stephen and Keiko at Tama shrine (though the physical occurs mainly in a dream). Stephen, in a sense, emerges from his writing and art to become a fuller person, realizing the limitations of painting and the pen in truly conveying life's beauty and pain: "There's something about being too perfect, that evenness which at times appears stiff, almost boring. I finally gave up after several tries" (170).

Summer: July 9, 1938-Summer: August 16, 1938

Summer: July 9, 1938 Summary

Matsu tells Stephen a story of a village where the plum rains never cease. The villagers there feel blessed by the rains' presence and fear that if the mist ever stopped, bad luck would find them. Stephen imagines spirits in the beach house garden and wishes for the sun.

Summer: July 16, 1938 Summary

Stephen gets his wish: blue sky has come to Tarumi. Tourists descend.

Matsu brings Stephen a letter from Pie. She is upset that another visit has been cancelled – it's been nearly a year since Stephen left. She has continued her secret volunteer work. She wonders how Stephen has changed and tells him that girls have come to the house asking after her handsome brother. Henry and Anne are still in Macao, and Pie and Mah-mee may visit them there.

Summer: July 25, 1938 Summary

In the afternoon heat, Stephen stops painting and goes to the cool woods where young Sachi once hid. He happens on Keiko, who has also fled there for the shade. They walk and speak, holding hands.

Summer: August 8, 1938 Summary

Matsu takes Stephen on a torch-lit trip to catch shrimp at a cove in the woods at dusk. Stephen hasn't seen Keiko since their last visit, and the spectacle of the leaping, squirming dinner is a welcome respite from Keiko's absence and the beach filled with tourists.

Summer: August 16, 1938 Summary

Matsu has made plans for the O-bon festival. His older sister Fumiko will visit from Tokyo, one of many returning home for a celebration of birthplace and ancestors. As the men wait for Fumiko in the crowd at the station, Stephen marvels that Matsu – such a solitary figure – is a son and a brother, and he is reminded again of the absence of other young men in town. He daydreams with homesickness of greeting his own family at the train. When Fumiko arrives, Stephen is struck by the wise, lined beauty of her face.

As Fumiko prepares lunch back at the house, she and Matsu talk about Tomoko. To Stephen, it is as if both of them become younger, speaking of their lost sibling. Fumiko tells Stephen that she had only just moved with her husband to Tokyo – where she thought Tomoko would one day join her – when Tomoko killed herself. She shares that she asked Matsu to come live in Tokyo but that "there has always been something or someone holding him here" (178). Stephen wonders why Matsu does not now make his relationship with Sachi known.

Summer: July 9, 1938-Summer: August 16, 1938 Analysis

The summer continues in these chapters, again a sort of punctuation between longer, more complex developments in the novel. Tourists descend, marking almost a year since Stephen arrived in Tarumi. He is no longer a stranger; rather, he has become in many ways a member of the village, close to Sachi, Matsu, Keiko, and others through their stories. The theme of isolation and connection has come full-circle – The outsider is now in many ways an insider, the unknown the known, the servant the served. When Matsu's sister Fumiko visits, Stephen realizes that he in fact knows more about Matsu's relationship than Matsu's own family does: Sachi is a secret, the "something or someone holding him here" (178), to Fumiko.

Summer: August 17, 1938-Autumn: September 23, 1938

Summer: August 17, 1938 Summary

Stephen wakes to the warm sounds and sight of Matsu and Fumiko preparing food to bring to the graves of the ancestors at the temple. As the trio walks there with the procession of villagers, Stephen thinks of Keiko and is glad not to see her; he does not wish to encounter her disapproving father again. Stephen remembers the Ghosts' Feast in Hong Kong, with its more elaborate headstones and the recognition of his mother's and father's families. They leave their offerings at the family plot, and Matsu steps away to visit Kenzo's grave.

When the three return to the village, it has been lit with colorful lanterns in many shapes. The mood is upbeat; the smell of food and the sound of music fill the air. Kenzo's teahouse remains silent; Stephen thinks of him and of Sachi, wondering if she will celebrate in Yamaguchi. He thinks of the Chinese being slaughtered by the Japanese and that there will be "no one left to celebrate them" (181).

Autumn: September 5, 1938 Summary

The garden begins to hint at the change of seasons, bringing a sense of the serious. Stephen writes, "maybe it's the light that gradually grows darker, making everything seem less trivial, forcing you to look harder to find your way" (185). The summer crowds have gone, and Tarumi is quiet again.

Stephen, feeling nostalgic for the days when fall meant returning to school, hears Matsu calling him from the garden. Matsu shows him a blooming kerria plant with yellow-orange flowers and tells him that it is a sign of good luck: normally, the plant blooms for only one week in the spring. Stephen asks Matsu if it means that they will have good luck; Matsu tells him that good luck will mean not having any bad luck.

Autumn: September 13, 1938 Summary

Stephen goes to the beach for the first time in weeks. After learning from Matsu that Keiko has been away with her family in Osaka, he anticipates her return. Pie has sent a postcard letting Stephen know that she and Mah-mee have visited Anne and Henry in Macao. Stephen thinks of these things as he walks among the detritus of the summer visitors – paper wrappers, a broken plastic shovel. He thinks of his own things left behind and the things he will have to leave in the future.

A flash appears in the distance. It is Keiko, running toward him, a new pendant around her neck glinting in the light. Stephen's joy turns to shock as she tells him that she will be unable to see him anymore, that "there can never be any 'us'" (187). The family has just learned that her brother was killed at Hsuchowfu in May. Stephen holds her as she sobs for her brother's loss and the loss of Stephen. Their eyes meet, then she turns and walks back over the dunes. That night, Stephen writes of the insanity of war, the dead on both sides, the scars left on everyone.

Autumn: September 16, 1938 Summary

Stephen dreams of Keiko running toward him and never being able to reach him. He longs to see her but does not. His heart aches for the colors of her hair, her clothes, the persimmons in her basket.

Autumn: September 23, 1938 Summary

A week of rain has stopped just in time for Shibun No-Hi, the Autumn Equinox. Matsu and Stephen take a muddy hike to Yamaguchi to celebrate with Sachi; when they arrive, they rinse off and put on robes. Stephen's body has filled out with his returned health and exercise.

As Sachi serves them a meal, Stephen notices Sachi's pleasure in feeding Matsu and Matsu's satisfaction that the house has stayed tight in the rain. In a sense Matsu – a servant at Stephen's grandfather's home – is the "master of the house" (190) here. But this sense is a double one Stephen remembers strongly from childhood: Ching, the family servant in Hong Kong, was powerful in her service. She was often more a household manager to Ba-Ba and a mother to the children than Mah-mee. The dynamics of friendship are visible as Sachi serves Matsu rice, Matsu tops off her tea, and Stephen lifts his bowl so that she won't have to reach for it.

Summer: August 17, 1938-Autumn: September 23, 1938 Analysis

As summer turns to autumn, these five chapters turn Stephen's eyes back to home: During a celebration of ancestors, he thinks of the war in China and wonders who will be left to celebrate the dead. A joyously late-blooming kerria plant in the garden continues the flower motif, offering good luck autumnally tempered by Matsu's answer to Stephen's question about it: "'As long as we don't have any bad luck" (185).

At the beach, Stephen has a final meeting with Keiko. She tells him that her brother has been killed in combat and that she and Stephen can never be together; her father, already unlikely to approve the union, will now never have to. Their grief for both losses is echoed in the surroundings Stephen has noted before her arrival on the sand: "paper wrappers, a plastic shovel... what used to be castles and moats.... I felt lonely seeing these things, not for those who'd left them, but for all the things I've had to leave" (186).

The trajectory of several of the novel's themes becomes evident. These "things I've had to leave" are becoming, for Steven, the texture of a life. He is beginning to understand that solitude and connection coexist; that beauty and suffering are sisters; and that the individual is always in some sense both part of a collective and totally on his or her own. While Stephen might have had a less-mature reaction to Keiko's rejection – perhaps longing for her in the garden – earlier in the novel, now he goes with Matsu to visit Sachi and finds happiness in their service to each other: "at the same time he poured more tea into her cup and there seemed to be a perfect balance. I knew neither of them would ever drift away from the other" (192). When

Sachi offers Stephen more rice in the next moment, he knows that he is as much a part of these lives as those who've lived them for decades.

Autumn: September 28, 1938-Autumn: October 19

Autumn: September 28, 1938 Summary

Stephen wakes feeling anxious and helps Matsu prune a black pine in the garden. Matsu asks if Stephen has stopped wanting to swim, and Stephen confides that his friendship with Keiko has ended. Cutting the pine, Matsu asks, "Isn't it interesting, Stephen-san… how sometimes you must cut away something in order to make it grow back stronger?" (193). Matsu goes on comparing human beings and plants, saying that all are part of nature and that humans can learn from it, that longer-lived humans encounter complications plants do not. He tells Stephen that if Keiko is important, she will remain with him, and that there will be many others. "No reason for you to quit swimming" (193), Matsu says.

Autumn: September 30, 1938 Summary

Stephen writes that the mail is slow; he has received nothing from Kobe or Hong Kong for a long time. Pie's birthday is next month, so he goes to Tarumi's general store to find a gift to send her. After having stayed away from town, he again hopes to see Keiko. He finds nothing for Pie at the store so buys some tinned foods to bring back to the house. As he leaves, two old men are speaking about the war. It amazes Stephen that they mention only Japanese victory, and not the incalculable Chinese losses.

Autumn: October 5, 1938 Summary

Stephen swims for the first time in weeks. The water has grown cold with the deepening of autumn. Back at the house, as Stephen takes a hot outdoor bath, Matsu arrives from the post office with a letter from Stephen's father and one from King.

King's letter is over two months old. He tells Stephen of the bombs, blackouts, and rationing in Canton and how they have scared the students at Lingnan away until only a handful are left. A childhood friend of theirs, Vivian Hong, has died in a bombing. He himself will be returning to Hong Kong soon and hopes to see Stephen there. He marvels at writing to Stephen in Japan, the source of so much misery in China. Stephen tries to remember Vivian and cannot. He longs for playing cricket and going to the movies with King back in Hong Kong, feeling that he belongs nowhere.

Ba-Ba's letter starts out with standard greetings and queries about Stephen's health. Farther along, Ba-Ba says that he will be taking a short trip from Kobe to Tokyo and asks if Stephen would like to join him.

Autumn: October 11, 1938 Summary

Stephen responds by letter that he would like to join his father in Tokyo; a telegram from Kobe confirms the trip. Stephen recalls a childhood memory of a trip alone with his father, or perhaps an uncle or a servant. He was fearful in a teeming marketplace and pulled along by a large hand, knowing "only that it was big and warm as it pulled me away from any harm" (197-8).

Autumn: October 19, 1938 Summary

Matsu and Stephen have visited Sachi in Yamaguchi for Stephen to say goodbye before his trip. Matsu accompanies Stephen into Tarumi for the train to Kobe; from there, Stephen and his father will go to Tokyo for three days. Matsu gives Stephen Fumiko's phone number and address in case of emergency.

As Stephen rides the train toward Kobe, away from Tarumi for the first time in more than a year, he remembers a childhood trip with his family to Tokyo and wonders what he and Ba-Ba will talk about for three days.

Ba-Ba meets Stephen at the Kobe station, and Stephen carries his father's valise. Stephen notices that there are more soldiers than there were the year before; they eye him and his father. The two have coffee before boarding the train for Tokyo, and Stephen shows Ba-Ba his arm – he has put on weight and is feeling well.

Autumn: September 28, 1938-Autumn: October 19 Analysis

At the beginning of these chapters, Stephen helps Matsu prune a black pine in the garden. This is perhaps the strongest example of the flower/flora motif in the novel, and the pine, along with other nearby plants in the garden, becomes a metaphor unpacked by Matsu: "Isn't it interesting, Stephen-san... how sometimes you must cut away something in order to make it grow back stronger?" (193). Nowhere is the novel more explicit about its meaning than in these chapters, from this observation to Matsu's "We aren't so different, humans beings and plants. We are all a part of one nature and from each other we learn how to live" (192).

The war is changing everything, and Stephen's time in Tarumi will soon be over. His exit from Tarumi begins with a short trip to Tokyo with his father. The mail is often delayed by the war (a letter from King is more than two months old), and Stephen's family is increasingly eager for him to return home. The Tokyo visit serves as a bridge between Stephen's time in Tarumi and the next stage of his life, when he will digest what he has learned and move forward a different person. He has a memory of himself as a child, being led through a crowd by an older man; we can see that Stephen, who has come to terms with his father's very human combination of strength and fallibility as a man, must take his own hand through life. The setting of Tokyo – the first new one in real time since the beginning of the novel – is important for the theme of the individual vs. the collective as Tokyo is the capitol of Japan, the center of Japanese nationalism. Stephen and his father will visit it as outsiders who do not belong.

Autumn: October 20, 1938-Autumn: October 26, 1938

Autumn: October 20, 1938 Summary

Stephen marvels at the enormity, sights, and sounds of Tokyo. He and his father stay in a hotel near the Ginza, a flamboyant commercial street. The Japanese military is omnipresent. Stephen walks to the Imperial Palace, the home of the emperor for whom so many are willing to fight and die.

The men have dinner at a restaurant famous for its marinated eel. During the meal, Stephen's father speaks Japanese: the other patrons, local, are discussing the war, and Chinese would turn heads. Ba-Ba suggests that Stephen return to Hong Kong before Christmas, and Stephen asks if it is safe. "'For now it is,'" answers Baba, "this time in Chinese" (201).

Autumn: October 22, 1938 Summary

While Stephen and his father are at lunch, they learn that Canton has fallen the day before. Stephen imagines the people there, exhausted by the constant bombing, surprised by the Japanese army landing in Bias Bay. The Japanese in the restaurant cheer, and Ba-Ba says that it is time to go. On the way to the train station, Stephen feels that he is being watched.

Stephen stays the night at his father's apartment in Kobe, then returns to Tarumi by train. Matsu meets him at the station. Stephen is glad to have spent time with his father, who seemed noticeably older. It's been decided that Stephen will sail to Hong Kong in the next week or so alone while his father bides his time in Kobe, finishing business and waiting to see what will happen next in the war. Matsu says, "I thought as much" (203).

Autumn: October 24, 1938 Summary

Stephen has not yet left, and already he's begun to miss Tarumi. As Matsu prepares dinner, the men hear on the radio that Japan has taken Hankow. Matsu turns it off and asks Stephen if he'd like to visit Sachi the next day. Stephen can barely answer, and does. Matsu tells Stephen that he should visit Sachi alone.

Autumn: October 25, 1938 Summary

Stephen has dreamt of Sachi the night before; in his dream she was bandaged, ill, and alone. Today, he finds her in her garden and gives her a vase he bought for her in Kobe. He tells her that he will be leaving soon. "Perhaps if the gods smile upon us, Stephen-san, we will have the chance to meet again" (204), she responds. They rake the stones in the garden, and Stephen tells Sachi that he worries about her – What if something should happen to Matsu? Sachi tells him that either she or Matsu might go first, and that she would do her best to continue living her life.

Sachi tells Stephen that he has given her and Matsu the one thing they lacked: a son. She confides in him that long ago, she and Matsu had a stillborn boy. Shocked and saddened, Stephen goes inside the house with Sachi. She gives him a gift in return for his: Tomoko's two stones. Stephen memorizes Sachi's face before he must say goodbye, possibly permanently: "she was still very beautiful. Then when her face slowly faded in the darkening shadows of late afternoon, I began to grieve" (206).

Autumn: October 26, 1938 Summary

Stephen spends the whole day at the beach, swimming and thinking of his adjustment to the quiet of Tarumi and the adjustment he will have to make to the noise of Hong Kong. He imagines staying in Tarumi, caring for Matsu and Sachi, a simple life. Feeling lonely, he hears something over the dunes. Unlike the times before, it is not Keiko who appears but Matsu, bringing lunch.

Autumn: October 20, 1938-Autumn: October 26, 1938 Analysis

In the first two of these chapters, Stephen visits the Imperial Palace in Tokyo, and he and his father eat in Japanese restaurants, where it becomes clear that they are fish out of water: the locals discuss the war in glowing terms, and Ba-Ba speaks in Japanese in order not to turn heads. Here, food, for most of the novel described in happy, grounding images, becomes an occasion for bleaker insight and a flight: "I watched my father look up from his plate sadly" (202). The men decide to leave – Stephen for Tarumi and goodbyes, his father for Kobe to finish business there.

Stephen visits Sachi in Yamaguchi a final time alone. She gives him the final piece of the puzzle that is her relationship with Matsu: she and Matsu, long ago, had a stillborn son. Her revelation is also the explication of her, Matsu, and Stephen's bond: "You have been the *musuko* we lost so many years ago" (205). She gives Stephen Tomoko's stones, a symbol of enduring hope. During a final visit to the beach, Stephen hears someone coming nearer across the dunes; it is Matsu. Whereas before Stephen might have been disappointed, he is now glad to see his friend: this is far less a traditional love-and-loss romance than it is the story of a young man becoming an empathetic citizen of the world.

Autumn: October 27, 1938-Autumn: October 29, 1938

Autumn: October 27, 1938 Summary

As Stephen packs for his journey to Hong Kong, three days away, he and Matsu feel their looming separation: "it's as if the house is slowly becoming a stranger to us. Matsu stares hard into each room as if he already sees it as it once was, silent and uncluttered" (207). Sachi turns up for an afternoon visit and stays until evening, an unexpected delight tinged with sadness. As Matsu walks her back to Yamaguchi, Stephen realizes that the visit was for Matsu, not for him.

Autumn: October 28, 1938 Summary

On the morning of Stephen's last full day in Tarumi, Matsu greets him with two packages. One contains dinner, Matsu tells him. The other is a secret.

Stephen gives Matsu his painting of the garden and thanks him for taking care of him. Matsu is deeply touched and responds, "I sometimes think it has been the other way around" (208).

They go to the Tama shrine, where Stephen performs the rituals from before. But he has not come to pray; rather, he wishes to leave a slip of paper on the wall near the altar with all of the other villagers' prayers so that something of him will remain.

Autumn: October 29, 1938 Summary

Stephen writes of his final dinner in Tarumi with Matsu the night before, his anxiousness, and Matsu's apparent calm. Stephen tells Matsu that he might take classes in Hong Kong; Matsu says that he might visit Fumiko in Tokyo and might move to Yamaguchi to be with Sachi.

After dinner, Matsu shows Stephen the *daruma* doll Stephen gifted him months before with one eye drawn in. "When you return, I'll draw in the other" (209), Matsu says.

On his last morning in Tarumi, Stephen sits in the garden and remembers the relationships that have blossomed there. He hears a sound at the gate and goes to it: Keiko has left a single, pressed white flower.

In the afternoon, Stephen and Matsu walk to the station. Foreboding rainclouds darken the sky, and the waves are strong. By the time they reach the station, it's begun to rain. As they prepare to part, Matsu bows low to Stephen. Instead of bowing in return, Stephen waits for Matsu to straighten, then hugs him. Matsu returns the embrace. Matsu assures Stephen that they will write and that he will continue to care for Sachi. As Matsu leaves, Stephen feels the urge to run after him.

On the train, Stephen finds the secret package from Matsu tucked into his baggage. In it are two blank-paged black leather books: "then as the train rattled toward Kobe, taking me away from Tarumi, I took out my fountain pen, opened one of the books, and began to write" (211).

Autumn: October 27, 1938-Autumn: October 29, 1938 Analysis

These three chapters are Stephen's final three days in Tarumi. Sachi visits the beach house – a surprise after Kenzo's suicide. It's clear that this visit, unlike some before, is more for Matsu than for Stephen: Matsu feels the loss of Stephen as much as Stephen feels the loss of him and Sachi, and Sachi is there to ease the transition.

Stephen gives his painting of the garden to Matsu. While this painting has not been mentioned many times in the novel, it is an important symbol of Stephen's transition: he has moved away from painting and writing primarily to express himself and toward using his gifts to serve others. When Matsu bows in gratitude, Stephen says, "It isn't half as good as having the real garden, but I thought you might enjoy it anyway" (208). Stephen has come out from behind his book and brush to experience real life with others. He has grown stronger not only in body, but also in mind.

When Stephen and Matsu visit Tama shrine one last time, Stephen leaves a prayer slip on the wall near the altar: "I wanted to leave a message on the wall by the altar, tacked alongside all the other hopeful requests so that even if I never returned to Tarumi, something of me would remain" (209). The theme of present and past returns: Stephen's present in Tarumi is quickly becoming his past, and he wishes to leave a bit of himself in the place that has given him so much. Like all of the prayer slips there, his holds a secret. We are never told what he writes in it.

Just before Stephen leaves for the train with Matsu, he finds a white flower on the garden gate from Keiko. Her flower motif has returned, a final gift of grace to commemorate their time together. A greater gift, though, and the one that brings the novel both back to its beginning and to its close, is Matsu's gift of two bound leather books. Stephen, changed and fortified by his time in Tarumi, will now create his next journey.

CHARACTER ANALYSIS

Stephen Chan

Stephen is the novel's protagonist and the author of his own journey in first-person journal form. He is a good-looking 20-year-old Chinese painter, writer, and student who, at the urging of his upper-middle-class parents, leaves school in Canton to spend a year recuperating from an undisclosed illness at his family's beach house in Tarumi, Japan.

When we meet Stephen, he has been ill for a long while and feels isolated by his recuperation. His complaints are those of a young man – not narcissistic, but a bit self-involved: he misses his school friends and is weary of time in bed. His sense of isolation deepens in Tarumi, becoming one both personal and cultural as the Second Sino-Japanese War escalates. He comes to see that there is far worse suffering than his own as he gets to know Matsu and Sachi and their stories of leprosy, loss, suicide, service, and transcendence.

Stephen starts out being a recorder of experience but moves into full participation in life as the novel continues. From falling in love to rescuing the village of Yamaguchi from fire, he begins not only to heal, but also truly to live in his own body and mind. At the beginning of the novel, he is frustrated by life's dualities. By the end, he comes to see that beauty and suffering, isolation and connection, the individual and the collective, and the present and the past really are one.

Matsu

Like his father before him, Tarumi villager Matsu is a lifelong servant of Stephen's family, caretaker of their summer home in Tarumi. He is about 60, stocky, with gray hair. He is a man of few words and at first seems impermeable to Stephen. As their friendship deepens, Matsu humbly reveals his history in Tarumi: how leprosy visited the village, how he saved Sachi, his sister Tomoko's suicide, his friendship with Kenzo. Matsu's relationship with Sachi is central to the novel – its layers of romantic love, friendship, suffering, service, and beauty are a roadmap and book of life to Stephen during his journey. Matsu's garden is a canvas on which many events of the novel are painted, and its flora often work as metaphor.

Sachi

Sachi is a former Tarumi villager and Matsu's longtime love and mother of their stillborn child. She is a traditional Japanese beauty scarred by leprosy, and her veil is symbolic of her shame. As a young woman, she was engaged to Kenzo. She was innocent and entitled. When she was struck with disease, she attempted to end her life by seppuku in order not to dishonor her family and fiancé. She found herself unable to complete the ritual, wanting to die but also wanting to live. Matsu helped her flee to Yamaguchi and ultimately, to thrive there. For Stephen, she is an example of beauty as truth – her scars and experiences make her breathtaking and unique. Stephen learns about empathy and strength via her journey from tragedy to wisdom. In her, he sees that suffering is not something to be struggled against and that it may become part of the texture of a sublime life. Like Matsu's garden, hers works both literally and metaphorically, showing how life may stand like a stone and flow like water at the same time. She embodies the theme of isolation and connection.

Kenzo

Kenzo, Matsu's childhood friend, is the third in the Matsu-Sachi-Kenzo triangle. As an arrogant young man, he was engaged to Sachi. He abandoned her when she informed him of her leprosy, the same disease which took Matsu's younger sister Tomoko. While he has remained loyal as a friend, his resentment and shame have followed him his whole life. After finding Sachi and Matsu in the garden at the beach house, he hangs himself.

Tomoko

Tomoko, Kenzo's younger sister, was, like Sachi, one of the finest girls in Tarumi. She committed seppuku with her father's fishing knife when she contracted leprosy. Her death impacted Matsu, Kenzo, and Sachi deeply. The two stones which were hers and become Stephen's are a gift of hope passed down through the novel.

Fumiko

Fumiko, Matsu's older sister, moved to Tokyo with her husband just before Tomoko's death. She visits Matsu and Stephen in Tarumi in the present day and is the catalyst for storytelling.

Ba-Ba

Ba-Ba, Stephen's father, is a Westernized businessman who wears spectacles and a suit. His family lives in Hong Kong, where he requires his children to understand and succeed in an increasingly global world. He stays mainly in Kobe, Japan, at his apartment on business. There, he is having an affair. He is loving but unapologetic, believing himself to be doing the right thing for all. Stephen's relationship with him moves from obedient admiration to resentment to acceptance as Stephen grows into being his own man.

Mah-mee

Mah-mee is a traditional upper-middle-class Chinese mother. Her relationship with Stephen is loving and protective but somewhat distant; her servant Ching does most of the daily work of child-rearing as Mah-mee plays mah-jongg and attends parties. She is blindsided by Ba-Ba's affair and leans on Stephen for information and support, somewhat reversing the parent-child relationship and forcing Stephen toward adulthood.

Pie

Stephen's twelve-year-old sister Pie is smart, wide-eyed, and pigtailed. She dotes on Stephen and writes to him while he is away in Tarumi. Like Stephen, she has a transformation as the war continues – unbeknownst to Mah-mee, she steps away from her life of attending the cinema and shopping and becomes a volunteer with refugees in Hong Kong.

Anne and Henry

Stephen's older sister Anne and older brother Henry attend school in Macao. They are not central to the novel, but their characters do reveal the family's Westernization and their separation during wartime.

Ching

Ching, the Chan family's servant, underlines the theme of service as both isolating and connecting. While she is not the Chan children's mother, she functions as such. It is she who nurses Stephen during his illness in Hong Kong, she who takes care of the family's every daily need. In her service are both humility and power. Her character has parallels with Matsu's and with Sachi's as they serve Stephen and each other.

King

King, Stephen's school friend, provides information about Stephen's school days and his position as a popular, handsome boy. Stephen's nostalgia for his friend adds to the theme of isolation and connection. King's letters to Stephen in Tarumi– increasingly delayed – bring news of the Japanese encroachment in China.

Keiko

Keiko, associated with floral sights and smells, is a graceful Tarumi girl with whom Stephen has a relationship during his recuperation. Her father does not approve of Stephen, seeing him as an unwelcome outsider (Chinese in Japan during the war, when Keiko's brother is away fighting). Keiko is drawn to Stephen but ultimately rejects him as her father's disapproval will not allow them to be together. She is a catalyst for Stephen's growth: first, she provides him connection in his isolation; then, her loss teaches him that beauty is both ephemeral and eternal. Her sister Mika acts mostly as an appendage, helping Keiko to approach Stephen.

Hiro

Hiro is one of the early Yamaguchi villagers. He helped Sachi during her transition there, helped Matsu build the village, and helps Stephen and Matsu put out the fire. His death heralds change.

Michiko

Michiko is another early Yamaguchi villager. Her personal care for Sachi during her first days and months in Yamaguchi taught Sachi about humility, empathy, and loss. Her fictionalized yet autobiographical story (told to Sachi and recounted to Stephen) of the pearl diver and her daughter is a story within a story within a story that underlines the theme of service (she gave up her daughter to save her) and parallels Matsu and Sachi's loss of a child.

THEMES

Isolation and Connection

Several of Tsukiyama's themes in *The Samurai's Garden* work on the concept of duality. Stephen begins his journey struggling with duality and, by the end of it, understands that embracing duality is embracing life. When he comes to Tarumi, he is isolated from his family, his friends, and to some degree (because he does not know himself fully) himself. He longs for connection but is unsure how to create it.

While Stephen was not a brute prior to this journey, he was in some senses still a boy. Through his relationships with Matsu, Sachi, and Keiko, he learns how to give and receive evolved compassion and kindness. He connects with others' history and suffering. As he leaves Tarumi on his own to embark on the rest of his life, he understands that all beings are both alone and together, and that the wisdom that comes from solitude may be applied to the relationships that make life worth living.

The Individual vs. The Collective

Tsukiyama, the novel's author, was born in San Francisco to a Japanese father and a Chinese mother. Her understanding of these two cultures is not only theoretical, but also personal. Her own life is informed by her parents' ancestry; we cannot know her mind, but it is not outlandish to imagine that her subjects explore cultural conflicts and convergences related to those she herself may have experienced.

Japanese nationalism stormed through China during the Second Sino-Japanese War; the imperialist Japanese government saw conquering China as its divine right. The Chinese during this period also held fast to their sense of national identity, clinging to tradition even as some Chinese fetishized the Western world. It is no wonder, considering, that individuals like Stephen in the novel feel swept along by forces larger than themselves. From young Japanese men feeling bound to join the army to the protagonist, Chinese and assimilating in the country he resents for attacking his own, the individual is both drawn to and wounded by the collective.

This theme intersects with the theme of isolation and connection, for the collective is not always evil; groups of people can work for good, as Pie does with her fellow Red Cross volunteers. Ultimately, Stephen returns to his homeland, embracing another duality: he returns to his nation, his roots, but he does so with the knowledge that the Japanese are people, not monsters; he knows some of them better than he knows his own family.

Present and Past

The novel's third duality-based theme, present and past, overarches the other two duality-based themes. When he comes to the beach house, Stephen is tied to his past and unsure about his present. Through his growing friendships with Matsu and Sachi and the revelations about his father (the affair), Stephen learns that history is always present, that the present is not separate from but predicated on the past, and that in fact, sometimes the past is more present than the present. As Sachi and Matsu share their history and Stephen faces what has been hidden in his own, he is able to encounter others more fully, to hold on to what is important, and to let go what is not. He is then ready to step into his future.

Suicide

The theme of suicide in *The Samurai's Garden* is both culturally specific and psychologically general. Ritual seppuku, honor suicide in the face of shame, is a Japanese concept going back centuries. But the larger idea of suicide as a response to shame and other dark emotions is broadly human. Stephen does not carry a great deal of shame, but he is certainly uncomfortable with his father's valuation of his painting as mere hobby. And at times, he feels guilt that – unlike friends back home or the young Japanese men from the village – he is unable to fight in the war. He has dark moments when he considers his isolation and the state of the world.

Stephen is not suicidal, but suicide seems interested in him: the shock of others' suicides becomes personal for Stephen in Tarumi. Tomoko and Kenzo (by hanging, not seppuku) sacrifice themselves to unhappiness and duty. Sachi narrowly avoids this fate. Against this backdrop, Tarumi's daily thrills and pleasures – friendship, romantic love, artistic creation, even just good food or a bracing swim – make life seem precious and worth living. By absorbing the wisdom of those around him who make peace with their darkness and learning from those who could not, Stephen comes into his own as a man confident about his ability to have transparent relationships with others and thrive in the world.

Service

Ching serves the Chan family. Matsu serves Stephen. Sachi serves Matsu and Stephen. Matsu serves Sachi. Stephen begins to see that service is as much strength as it is humility, and in the end, he serves Matsu, Sachi, and others around him.

Before Tarumi, Stephen's upper-middle-class upbringing caused him to see Ching in roles: at times an employee, at times a mother. One-on-one with Matsu at the beach house, he is encouraged by circumstance to see this "servant" as a complete, complex human being with far more to his actions than the providing of mundane physical comforts.

In fact, Matsu's service is ultimately that of the novel's title's "samurai": he is a protector from a place of great love, fallen on his sword for the betterment of Sachi, for whom he fights. Matsu has given up the prospect of a traditional married life in order to make a life for Sachi. She has returned the gift by devoting herself in whatever ways she can to Matsu's happiness. By slowly revealing the true nature of their relationship, the servant-samurai and the leper show Stephen how he might become a samurai his own and only life.

SYMBOLS AND MOTIFS

Weather and Seasons

The Samurai's Garden is structured by seasons and their weather. Stephen's "chapters" are dates in his journal headed by season (Spring, Summer, Autumn, Winter). Stephen often writes about his challenges and changes in terms of seasons: "All through the thick, sticky summer, the heat made things worse" (3), and seasonal archetypes abound, with spring as rebirth, summer as fruition, autumn as loss and change, and winter as death. In the first "Winter" chapter, Stephen writes, "Sachi's presence, which had held us and the garden captive is gone, leaving an emptiness that can't be filled" (73).

Weather – from balmy days to horrible storms – often reflects characters' inner lives. When a storm hits Tarumi just after Stephen learns of his father's infidelity, he and Matsu are pummeled by the torrential rain and waves: "The wall of water swept us both off our feet, knocking us solidly against the house" (52). Stephen has been knocked down psychologically, and the physical wave embodies that shock, making his inner and outer lives one.

Flora (Especially Flowers) and The Garden

Throughout the novel, flowers are associated with grace and good luck. Keiko often has a lavender scent, and most of Stephen's interactions with her involve flowers: "I looked up to see a shower of white petals fall in my direction… I jumped up and could hear two girls laughing aloud as I rushed to the gate" (19). Keiko is also associated with persimmons, fruit that comes from a flower, colorful and abundant. Sachi and Matsu both find plants flowering against odds or out of season in their gardens. Stephen, on

Sachi's balloon plant's blooms, may as well be asking about Sachi herself in Yamaguchi: "'How are they able to grow here?' I asked, amazed that anything so delicate could grow among rocks" (127). Matsu, using the Japanese word for "flower," calls Sachi his "[l]ittle hana" (59).

The garden at the center of the novel changes with weather and the seasons as the lives of the characters change. It blooms, goes dormant, is wrecked by storm, and returns. Its transformations show how fragility and resilience may coexist. When Matsu, Sachi, and Stephen work in either the main garden or Sachi's stone garden, their time there is also work on the soul. When Matsu resists Stephen helping in his garden after the storm, "Sachi turned to Matsu and softly said, 'I remember a time when you told me working in the garden would give me back my life'" (56). Matsu then allows Stephen to join them in rebuilding.

Food

Tsukiyama uses food throughout the novel as a grounding trope, with a few exceptions (e.g., Stephen and his father eating in Tokyo as they are watched by wary Japanese patrons). From the comfort of a first breakfast with Matsu ("rice with pickled vegetables and miso soup" (13)) to the joy of the "[h]omemade yokan" Keiko gives Stephen (Matsu comments, "'You must be quite special to this girl'" (61)), food connects people to places and each other.

Stephen's Painting and Book

Stephen's painting and writing allow him to capture on canvas and paper his surroundings and, more importantly, his feelings. His journal literally and figuratively holds his Tarumi experience. His painting of Matsu's garden from the novel's title is his final gift to Matsu, encapsulating all he has learned there and modeling service. Matsu's final gift to Stephen, two blank books, is the tabula rasa on which Stephen will write his future.

Prayer Slips

The prayer slips at Tama shrine are mentioned only twice in the novel – once on Stephen's first visit there, once on his last. But these visits and the slips frame Stephen's time in Tarumi. They show that he has moved from being an outsider to having an investment in Tarumi and its people. They show that he has learned to bridge isolation and connection, past and present, the individual and the collective: "I knew all the praying in the world wouldn't stop the war… or make my parents love each other again. I wanted to leave a message… something of me would remain" (209).

Sachi's Veil

When Stephen and Sachi first meet, she is wearing a black veil to cover her face, which has been scarred by leprosy. Stephen gets glimpses of her face beneath and finds her beautiful both in spite of and because of the scars. For the young artist, this realization that beauty occurs not just in the obvious but in the "ugly" is central. It ripples into all of his relationships.

The veil is at once a symbol of shame and – when Sachi removes it – a window into vulnerability. When she shows her true face, she bares her history and her soul. Stephen spots Sachi outside Kenzo's funeral: "she lifted her veil and her eyes caught mine for just a moment as she bowed low in my direction" (110). Here, Sachi reveals herself to Stephen both literally and figuratively. Stephen has just been shamed by Keiko's father, and though his friend is not aware of that encounter, she lifts the veil on shame for both of them.

Tomoko's Stones

Like the veil and the prayer slips, Tomoko's stones are not frequently present in the novel. However, they are a powerful talisman of Tomoko's story and the larger story of Tarumi. When Tomoko collected them, the stones were youthful good luck. In Sachi's hands, they are remembrance of a friend torn away by disease and tradition. Sachi gives them to Stephen as he prepares to leave Tarumi: "in the palm of my hand Sachi placed Tomoko's two shiny black stones, collected so many years ago for their magic powers" (205). Now, the stones are magic, but not as in a young girl's imagination. Instead, they hold the wonder of Stephen's own transformation.

IMPORTANT QUOTES

1. "I wanted to find my own way, so this morning I persuaded my father to let me travel alone from his apartment in Kobe to my grandfather's beach house in Tarumi." (Autumn: September 13, 1937, Page 3)

   Stephen does indeed want to find his own way. Here he points to the actual trip between Kobe and Tarumi (his father's home and the one that will become Stephen's for a year). But he also hints at the natural separation that must occur between a boy and his father as that boy becomes a man.

2. "Stepping through the bamboo gate, I found myself in the garden. The sweet perfumes were immediately intoxicating. A silk tree, still heavy with summer blossoms, and two large black pine trees shaded the house. An oval-shaped pond, with hints of movement that flashed orange and silver beneath its surface, dominated one side of the garden. It was surrounded by pale green moss. A wooden bridge arched across its width, and lines of odd-shaped, waterworn stones created two paths, one leading through the secluded garden right up to the front door, while the other disappeared around the back of the house. White sand formed soft beds in the crevices." (Autumn: September 13, 1937, Pages 9-10)

   This is Stephen's first moment in the samurai's garden, rich in image and metaphor. He will live and work there; paint there; begin to fall in love there; witness the relationships between Matsu, Sachi, and Kenzo there; and finally leave there having re-created it on canvas and gifted it to Matsu, its creator.

3. "With each stroke against the salty water, I felt a new surge of energy travel through my body. I swam back and forth, my arms thrusting forward with each stroke as I disrupted the calm of the sea with my furious motions. The coolness of the water felt good against my body. As I relaxed, a sense of freedom emerged which had been buried under my illness." (Autumn: September 16, 1937, Page 14)

Stephen swims frequently at the beach in Tarumi. This ritual heals both his body and his mind. He finds freedom in the water and emerges from his illness into his new life. It is on the beach that he first meets Keiko; often, it is there that he reflects on his experiences among the people living beyond the dunes.

4. "'Japan is like a young woman who thinks too much of herself. She's bound to get herself into trouble.'" (Autumn: September 20, Page 17)

As Stephen and Matsu listen to the news on Matsu's radio, Stephen asks Matsu his opinion on Japanese encroachment in China. Matsu's response reveals Matsu's humanity: He is an individual, not an imperialist.

5. "For the first time in my life I saw what it meant to be a leper, a disgraced one. They seemed to watch me with just as much curiosity. I tried not to stare, but I couldn't take my eyes off their wounds; the missing fingers and toes, the large, gaping holes in the sides of their faces, the mangled features that had once been noses and ears. It looked as if they were all wearing monstrous masks that I kept waiting for them to remove." (Autumn: October 8, 1937, Page 25)

This is Stephen's first visit to Yamaguchi. The idea of the "monstrous mask" is important; it will be echoed in Kenzo's calling Sachi a "monster" when he finds her with Matsu in the garden. Stephen's journey will teach him that everyone wears a mask and that beauty is what dwells beneath it.

6. "While the left side of her face had been devastated, the unblemished right side was the single most beautiful face I'd ever seen." (Autumn: October 8, 1937, Page 27)

    Stephen is captivated by Sachi's strange beauty on their first meeting, and throughout the novel. While at first he struggles to reconcile her loveliness and her scars, soon he sees them as one and the same. He learns that beauty and suffering are two sides of the same coin.

7. "After Matsu left, I began to paint. I didn't want to lose the light which had already begun to change." (Autumn: October 21, 1937, Page 32)

    Stephen begins his painting of the garden, which will serve to encapsulate his time in Tarumi and will be his gift to the garden's samurai, Matsu. "[T]he light which had already begun to change" is at once literal and psychological: Stephen's perspective is being altered by the "light" of Tarumi.

8. "'Are there lots of young people around here now?' I continued. 'Not many. A few families in town,' she answered. 'Most of the young men have joined the army, while the others move to the city as soon as they can.'" (Autumn: October 29, 1937, Page 35)

Stephen speaks with Keiko on the beach. He learns that Tarumi has been depleted of young men for the Japanese army. This fact will become problematic for Stephen and Keiko: her father does not approve of the young Chinese man in his village while his son is off at war against China.

9. "In place of the greens, browns, and flashes of color which punctuated Matsu's garden, the spareness of Sachi's garden stunned me. There were no trees, flowers, or water, only a landscape made of sand, stones, rocks, and some pale green moss which covered the shaded areas." (Autumn: October 30, 1937, Page 40)

Stephen sees Sachi's stone garden for the first time. Hers works in tandem with Matsu's to provide meaning: there is beauty both in abundance and in simplicity. Her creation of it, with Matsu's encouragement, has helped her to heal her life.

10. "'Does Kenzo know Sachi?' I quickly asked. Matsu slowed down and turned to face me. 'Tarumi is a small place. We all knew each other when we were young.' 'Then why doesn't Kenzo go to visit her?' 'When we were young, Sachi cared a great deal for Kenzo, but the disease changed everything. After she left for Yamaguchi, she would no longer see him.'" (Autumn: November 19, 1937, Page 49)

Stephen has just met Kenzo at the teahouse. Here, he begins to understand the Matsu-Sachi-Kenzo triangle. The relationships have many layers, and Tsukiyama lifts them slowly, revealing the secret-keeping among the friends and the depth of their loyalty to one another.

11. "As my head cleared, I remembered the last thing I felt was the strong punch of the rushing water and then nothing; blackness. It was just a miracle that the house still stood, somehow having survived the crashing waves." (Autumn: November 24, 1937, Page 53)

Stephen has just received his mother's letter about his father's infidelity. He is reeling, and the storm embodies his shock and sense of helplessness. But Stephen ultimately finds himself resilient – like the house and his new friends.

12. "Each day I work in the garden with Sachi, I feel stronger. The headaches lose their urgency once my hands dig deep into the cool, dark soil and I smell the damp dirt and pine. Even the cold wind of approaching winter makes me feel more alive." (Autumn: November 30, 1938, Page 57)

Sachi has come down from Yamaguchi to help rebuild Matsu's garden. As fall turns to winter, Stephen gains strength through working with his friends. This togetherness, this mutual service, becomes a major element in Stephen's transformation.

13. "Sachi let out a small scream as her scarf dropped to the floor. For a split second, they all stood frozen; the white, puckered scars magnified in the bright light. Kenzo stepped back. 'You really are a monster!' he roared." (Autumn: December 1, 1937, Page 67)

When Kenzo finds Sachi with Matsu in the garden, he feels betrayed. His rage punches through the present to the past. Not long after this fight, Kenzo hangs himself, a sad parallel with the suicide Sachi was unable to perform on herself long ago.

14. "'Would you like to help?' she asked. 'I don't want to ruin the pattern,' I answered, as I stepped back and shrugged my shoulders. Sachi raised her right hand up to cover her laugh. 'How can you ruin stones, Stephen-san? You can only rearrange them, and who knows if it won't be for the better.'" (Winter: December 5, 1938, Page 77)

Stephen learns another existential lesson from Sachi and her garden. After the fight at the beach house, Sachi's raking reveals duality: stones are both fluid and immutable, like human beings. And change is inevitable – one may as well embrace it.

15. "I was old enough to understand everything he said, but as his mouth softly formed the words, I knew the sense of integrity I had long admired in him had died, and that I was already grieving for its loss." (Winter: December 6, 1937, Page 85)

Stephen's father visits Tarumi and discusses his affair. Stephen loves his father no less than before; he simply understands now that he is only human, and fallible. This is part of Stephen's progress toward manhood, grieving for innocence, and learning to parent himself.

16. "Above the counter, not more than three feet away from us, hung Kenzo's limp body." (Winter: February 4, 1938, Page 99)

Kenzo has hung himself after learning of Sachi and Matsu's ongoing relationship, unable to deal with his own resentment and shame. The theme of suicide – once part of the stories of the past – becomes horribly present.

17. "When her father turned back to me, it was with a look so full of hate I simply bowed my head and walked quickly away." (Winter: February 7, 1938, Page 109)

Keiko's father encounters Stephen at Kenzo's funeral and rejects him – the young Chinese man in a Japanese village in wartime – with utter contempt. Stephen, blossoming into himself, now knows what it is to be seen not as an individual but as a faceless enemy.

18. "By seventeen, I had shamed my family twice; first, when the disease chose me, and then when I was too weak to honor them with my death." (Spring: April 15, 1938, Page 131)

After the fire in Yamaguchi, Stephen spends time with Sachi, and she tells him the heart of her story from decades ago: How she came to the leper village after failing to commit seppuku. More layers of her relationship with Matsu are revealed, and her journey from suffering to peace is gets clearer.

19. "'What are you doing?' I asked. Matsu waited until the last turn of the wheel slowed, then came to a complete stop. He held up the knife so I could clearly see its ivory handle and honed blade. 'It was my father's fishing knife,' he said." (Spring: May 15, 1938, Page 158)

Matsu sharpens the very knife about which he's just told Stephen: the fishing knife his sister Tomoko asked him to help her find to commit seppuku after she contracted leprosy. Matsu refused then, but she found it and carried out her wish. The past overlays the present.

82

20. "All over Japan they were celebrating the dead, even as more and more Chinese were being slaughtered. There would be no one left to celebrate them." (Summer: August 17, 1938 Page 184)

Stephen celebrates O-bon with Matsu and Fumiko. While he has come to love his life in Tarumi, he worries increasingly about the war. The ancestors of the past and the dead of the present converge in Stephen's imagination.

21. "The madness of war destroyed much more than just the soldiers fighting in it. It picked apart everything in its way, so that no one escaped its clutches. Not even someone as decent and humane as Keiko would be left without scars." (Autumn: September 13, 1938, Page 188)

Stephen has encountered Keiko on the beach. As much as they desire each other, she must reject him or risk shaming her family. The war has affected everyone, and Stephen's "scars" will be like Sachi's, finally – a record of his feelings for Keiko, beauty in suffering.

22. "I'd always felt uncomfortable being waited on, even by Ching, who has worked for my family ever since I can remember. But it was evident that after so many years Ching had a certain power over our family." (Autumn: September 23, 1938, Page 191)

As Stephen witnesses Matsu and Sachi serving each other at dinner, he remembers Ching's service to his family. He has come to understand that service is not always servitude – it can be a relationship of power, even one of great depth.

83

23. "Sometimes we love and hate without thought. We expect too much from one another, and often we are wrong." (Autumn: September 28, 1938, Page 193)

   Matsu talks with Stephen as they prune the black pine in the garden, using the flora as metaphor. He could be speaking of almost any character in the novel, or of the Chinese and Japanese. The flip side of his assertion, of course, is that sometimes we are right, and we do great things for one another.

24. "You have been the musuko we lost so many years ago." (Autumn: October 25, Page 205)

   During a last visit with Stephen, Sachi reveals the final secret of her past with Matsu: they had a stillborn child. Stephen becomes that child to Sachi and Matsu. His connection with them is in some ways more familial than that with his biological family.

25. "Then as the train rattled toward Kobe, taking me away from Tarumi, I took out my fountain pen, opened one of the books, and began to write. (Autumn: October 29, 1938, Page 211)

   Having said goodbye to Matsu and Sachi, Stephen begins the journey home. Matsu's gift – two blank books – symbolizes Stephen's future. With all he has learned in Tarumi, he will write it.

ESSAY TOPICS

1. In The Samurai's Garden, Tsukiyama, a 21st-century woman, writes in first person as a man. Considering the cultural setting of the novel (1930s Japan during the Second Sino-Japanese War), why might she have chosen this narrator?

2. Stephen's book is his storytelling method. Why does Tsukiyama choose this means of expression for her narrator (vs. simply having him "speak" his thoughts, his feelings, and the novel's events)? Please consider Stephen's personality, the journal style's effect on the reader, and the importance of the act of creation as put forth in the novel.

3. Flowers are a central symbol in *The Samurai's Garden*. Please choose three instances of flowers as symbol from the novel and explain how they help us to understand Stephen's journey.

4. The theme of past and present gives *The Samurai's Garden* much of its emotional weight. Why does Tsukiyama give Stephen a fairly simple, innocent past in comparison with the pasts of Matsu, Sachi, and Kenzo? Please use examples from each character's past in your explanation.

5. Many readers reading this novel for the first time believe, when Stephen meets Keiko, that it will become a love story. Why does Tsukiyama first set up, then flout this expectation? What kind of story does it seem is more important to the author to explore, and why?

6. Matsu is the "samurai" in *The Samurai's Garden*. Please do some research into the Japanese tradition of

the samurai and find parallels in the novel's exploration of Matsu as a character. How is Matsu a "samurai"? Why does it matter, considering one or more of the novel's themes?

7. This novel is structured by seasons, from Autumn to Autumn during Stephen's stay in Tarumi. Breaking Stephen's stay into these seasons (Autumn, Winter, Spring, Summer, Autumn), how do you see the events of each season reflecting that season as archetype (e.g., Winter as death)?

8. The novel's suicides of the past – Tomoko's successful and Sachi's attempted – are never far from Matsu's, Sachi's, and Kenzo's minds. When Kenzo hangs himself in the present, what is his reason? Is he sending a message? Extinguishing shame with honor? Getting revenge? All, some, or none of the above? Please use Kenzo's own words and the words of others about him to support your answer.

9. To what degree do Stephen's nationality, his economic status, and his Westernization affect his ability to understand traditional Japanese Tarumi and assimilate with its villagers? What about Stephen is particularly "Chinese"? What about him is "Western"? What about him is more universal? Please use examples from the novel.

10. Why does Tsukiyama choose Matsu's garden as the subject of Stephen's painting (as opposed to, for example, Sachi, Tama shrine, Keiko, the beach, or any other subject)? How do the garden and Stephen's re-creation of it reflect Stephen's trajectory in the novel? Please use excerpts during which Stephen paints or

discusses painting, along with descriptions of the garden, as support.

Made in United States
North Haven, CT
19 September 2022

24300900R00049